Contents

1. Introduction ....
2. A (Very) Brief History of the ͟
3. The Main Parts of a Ukulele 12
4. Choosing a Ukulele 15
5. Playing Positions 20
   - *Holding Your Ukulele* 20
   - *Left Hand Playing Positions* 21
6. Tuning Your Ukulele 22
7. A Few Musical Terms Defined 25
8. First Chords 27
9. Chord Progressions and a First Song 30
10. Strumming Techniques 34
    - *(1) Thumb* 34
    - *(2) Index finger* 35
    - *(3) Picks/Plectrums* 35
11. Six Really Useful Strumming Patterns 37
    - *Strumming Pattern #1* 37
    - *Strumming Pattern #2* 39
    - *Strumming Pattern #3* 42
    - *Strumming Pattern #4* 44
    - *Strumming Pattern #5* 46
    - *Strumming Pattern #6* 49
12. Three Chord Tricks 52
13. Alternative Tunings 60
14. Moveable Chords 62
15. Percussive Strumming 67
    - *Percussive Method #1* 67
    - *Strumming Pattern #7* 67
    - *Percussive Method #2* 68
    - *Strumming Pattern #8* 69
    - *Strumming Pattern #9* 70
    - *Strumming Pattern #10* 70
    - *Percussive Method #3* 70

16. Rhythm Soloing 71
- *The Split Strum* 71
- *The Triple Strum* 73
- *Putting it All Together* 78

17. A Closer Look at Chords 79
- *Major Chords* 79
- *Minor Chords* 80
- *Seventh & 'major seventh' Chords* 81
- *Sixth Chords* 82
- *Minor Seventh Chords* 83
- *Ninth Chords* 83
- *Diminished and Augmented Chords* 85

18. Ukulele Chords 90

Songs

Hound Dog (Lieber/Stoller) 33
Blowin' in the Wind (Bob Dylan) 38
Teenage Kicks (J. O'Neill) 41
Folsom Prison Blues (Johnny Cash) 43
Bye Bye Love (F. Bryant/B. Bryant) 45
Maybe Baby (Hardin/Petty) 48
You've Got to Hide Your Love Away (Lennon/McCartney) 50
Putting On the Style (Lonnie Donegan) 77

A famous strummer!

Ukulele!

A Strummer's Guide

by

Jez Quayle

WARNING: Playing the ukulele can be extremely addictive

Jez Quayle

Published by Lulu.com

© 2013 Jez Quayle. All rights reserved.

www.youtube.com/ukulelejez

ISBN: 978-1-291-47893-8

All profits from sales of this book are being donated to Save the Children.

I'd like to thank the lovely Janoria Steele for her invaluable help in proof reading earlier drafts of this book, for assistance in formatting, and most importantly, for making many cups of tea for me whilst I was busy writing.

For Jan, with love.

1. Introduction

I was given a ukulele as a present by a musical uncle when I was eleven or twelve years old, and I've tinkered around on one ever since. I found the 'teach yourself' book I was given at the time pretty confusing though, and it didn't help me to get to grips with my treasured new instrument all that much. Nevertheless, I did learn three or four chords and a handful of simple little ditties, and I was pleased with how they sounded. But I didn't know where to go from there.

A couple of years later I was given a guitar, which became my main focus for a long time. After all, on the guitar you can play all sorts of music: punk, folk, rock 'n' roll, pop, country, etc., and on the 'uke' you can only play silly little songs like 'Little Brown Jug', 'Coming 'Round the Mountain', and musical hall tunes. Well, that's what I thought at the time.

In more recent times I've discovered the true versatility of the ukulele, as have many other players, both young and old. You can play any type of music on the uke! It may sound a little different, and you may look a little daft when you assume a legs-apart, low-slung, rockin' stance, but that's the charm of this amazing little instrument. Ukuleles just seem to make people smile!

In the 1950s there was the skiffle craze, and in the 1970s there was punk rock. These movements took music out of the hands of formally trained, flashy and virtuoso musicians, and gave it back to the likes of you and me. With just a handful of chords you could play great music, have fun, and get together with other like-minded individuals. You could even perform in public. I see the rise in popularity of the ukulele in recent times to be similar in some ways to punk and skiffle. I'm not suggesting that the ukulele represents a distinct musical movement or that there will be uke music at the top of the music charts each week, but the approach and attitude are similar. Ukulele players do it their own way, they play what they want, how they want, and because of the size of ukuleles, they can do it pretty much anywhere they want too.

Like the guitar in skiffle and punk, with just a handful of ukulele chords you can play loads of great songs. Unlike the guitar though, many ukulele chords can be played with just one or two fingers (and in a couple of cases, no fingers at all!) ...so, it can be really quick to learn. Also, songs that sound pretty average or like pale imitations of famous versions of songs on the guitar, suddenly take on a fresh, new guise when played on the ukulele ...and punk and skiffle are two types of music that I love to play and sound great on the ukulele too!

- Introduction -

Over the last ten years or so the ukulele's popularity has increased remarkably, such that most towns and cities now have one or two ukulele clubs where enthusiastic players get together to strum, sing and learn ukulele playing techniques from each other.

Until pretty recently, decent ukuleles were difficult to come by, at least in the UK. Nowadays, however, most musical instrument shops stock a reasonable range of ukes, from basic beginner's models to seriously expensive instruments; having said that, for the price of a pretty mediocre guitar you can still pick up an excellent ukulele.

It's hard to say why the ukulele has become so popular. I recall seeing former Beatles, Paul McCartney and George Harrison playing ukuleles on stage and on television in the mid 1990s and beyond. I thought they made it look pretty cool and fun, and that made me pick up my old uke a little more often. The Ukulele Orchestra of Great Britain has done much to bring the ukulele to people's attention too (see picture above). In their many live performances and television appearances they've demonstrated the uke's versatility, the fun that can be had playing a uke, and how uke's can not only be played solo, but also in ensembles.

A number of recent chart hits have featured the ukulele, such as Israel Kamakawiwo's (see picture on left) recording of 'Somewhere Over the Rainbow' and Train's 'Soul Sister'. These recordings have shown how the uke isn't just a toy, or a silly novelty instrument, but can be a serious musical device in the right hands. Perhaps the simplicity and accessibility of the ukulele appeal to those who get frustrated with the complexity and superficiality of modern life and the digital age? Who can be sure? I'm just glad I play one, and I'm glad many others do too. The ukulele is now starting to replace the recorder as the instrument that children are encouraged to play at school in the UK.

What's In This Guide?
First of all ...RELAX! If you've never touched a musical instrument before in your life, or were put off learning how to play one by the way music was taught to you at school, then I reckon this is the guide for you. I won't assume any prior musical ability or knowledge. To be honest, you don't need much to make a good sound on the ukulele. I'll define and explain any musical and technical terms you need to know. I promise there won't be any mentions of really hard stuff like 'crotchets', 'staves' and 'semibreves', anyway. You can learn that stuff

- Introduction -

later, if you want to. I won't be teaching you how to read music — I'll just help you to understand a bit about how it works.

If you work your way through the chapters slowly and carefully in the order in which they appear, and practice any new playing techniques and other material I present as directed, it won't be very long before you've gone from being a complete beginner to a pretty solid uke strummer. I won't be showing you how to play too much 'fancy stuff'. For example, I won't talk about finger-picking or playing instrumental solos using scales. I'll show you how to strum the ukulele so you can accompany yourself or others when singing great songs. As the title suggests, this is 'A Strummer's Guide'.

I begin by describing the main parts of a ukulele. You'll need a reasonable understanding of this before you can begin playing, and this knowledge will also help you when buying/choosing a ukulele. I'll describe the different ways of holding your ukulele so that you can play it easily and comfortably, and teach you how to tune your instrument by ear. Before proceeding any further, I give definitions of some key musical terms that I'll be using within the guide.

At this point, you'll be ready to learn your first 'chords' (I'll show you where to put your fingers and why). Throughout the guide there'll be pictures of my hands, showing what chords and playing techniques should look like – copy what you see in these pictures and you won't go far wrong.

Next, I'll explain how to put these first chords together, and give you some simple exercises that will help you to become familiar with the chords and changing between them. Pretty soon you'll be playing a first song. I'll describe different techniques for strumming your ukulele in a rhythmic fashion. You'll gently get to grips with all of these techniques by trying them out in a number of songs.

The songs presented in the guide have been chosen because they're well-known/popular, they illustrate the stuff I'm explaining nicely, they're not too difficult to play, and ...well ... I think they're just great songs. Along the way you'll pick up more chords, until you know enough to play dozens of songs. I explain how many great songs are constructed around just three chords, and how an understanding of this can help when learning new songs. Next, I describe how some players vary the ways in which they tune their ukuleles.

In the penultimate chapter, I explain how to create your own 'rhythm solos', using the chords you'll have learned together with some additional strumming techniques. Finally, for those who want to know more about chords and how they work, I present an account of how different types of ukulele chord are constructed and used.

- Introduction -

When describing ukulele playing techniques I refer to the actions undertaken by the left and right hands as if readers are all right-handed. This is done to keep descriptions as simple and concise as possible, and not because I have anything against left-handed people (my son is sinistral). If you are amongst that number, then please consider references to the right hand to mean 'strumming hand', and references to the left hand to mean the 'neck/fingering hand'. You do get a special mention from time to time folks.

Take your time, follow the directions and advice I give, and practice, practice, practice (there's no substitute for it!). But practice doesn't have to be boring exercises – it can simply be playing songs or techniques that you like over and over, either by yourself or with others who play the uke or other instruments.

A marauding crowd of jolly, ukulele wielding zombies?
No – the first British Ukulele Festival – Cheltenham, 19th June, 2010

2. A (Very) Brief History of the Ukulele

The Hawaiian word 'ukulele' roughly translates as "jumping flea". This perhaps refers to the instrument's size and associations with fun times. Or perhaps the name is a metaphor for the movements of a uke player's fingers. Legend also suggests 'ukulele' was the nickname of the Englishman Edward William Purvis, who was one of King Kalākaua's officers: he was small, had a fidgety manner, and was an expert uke player.

The ukulele is a late nineteenth century adaptation of a small guitar-like instrument called the 'Machete' that was taken to Hawaii by Portuguese immigrants. By various routes, the ukulele travelled over to the USA, and in the 1920s there was a ukulele boom there, particularly amongst those who dreamed of the pacific island paradise from which the instrument emerged. Between then and the 1940s the ukulele remained popular, but became more associated with jazz and popular American music than idyllic Hawaiian beaches. In the 1930s the uke was famously played by musicians such as Cliff 'Ukulele Ike' Edwards and Roy Smeck.

In the UK we've tended to associate the ukulele with 1920s and 1930s music hall, and in particular, singer and comedian, George Formby, whose light and occasionally 'saucy', comical songs helped to boost the morale of the British nation during the second world war (see picture on left). A couple of Formby's songs were banned by the BBC due to their suggestive lyrics (nice one George!). Instead of a standard ukulele, however, Formby usually played the louder and brasher sounding 'banjo ukulele', which is a hybrid of the ukulele and banjo (sometimes called a 'banjolele').

Ukuleles remained fairly popular in Britain until the mid 1950s. In fact, they were such a main stream instrument at that time that sheet music for popular songs usually showed ukulele chords above the lyrics and melody, and not guitar chords as they do today. With the skiffle craze and the advent of rock 'n' roll, however, guitars became the coolest things to own and play for any budding young musician (typically males). After that, ukuleles tended not to be taken too seriously. Compared to guitars they were small, quiet, old fashioned, ...and just not ...well ...cool ...daddio.

Thankfully, this has ALL changed, and the uke is now back with a vengeance ...well, four strings and a small body ...ukes ARE cool AND sexy ...and EVERYONE is playing them ...well, a little exaggeration never hurt anyone, eh!?

3. The Main Parts of a Ukulele

Before learning to play the ukulele it's useful to know what the main parts of the instrument are called, as I'll be referring to these parts from time to time.

The Strings
There are four of these, and they're usually made of nylon. They're often referred to as the 1st, 2nd, 3rd, and 4th.

The 1st string is the thinnest and makes the highest note.

The 2nd string is thicker and makes a lower note than the 1st.

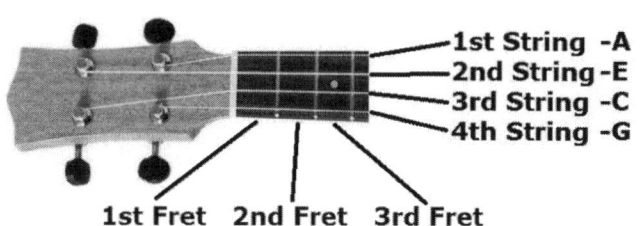

The 3rd string is thicker than the 2nd and makes a lower note than the 1st and 2nd strings.

On most string instruments the strings get progressively thinner like this from the 1st string onwards. However, on the ukulele, the 4th string is usually thinner and makes a higher note than the 3rd and 2nd strings. This is referred to as 're-entrant' tuning, and is partly what gives the ukulele its distinctive sound.

The four strings are also referred to by the notes they make in the standard, re-entrant 'C tuning'. From the 4th to the 1st these are: G C E A. Some players use different tunings (see chapter on 'Alternative Tunings').

The Headstock (sometimes called the 'head')
If you are right-handed, then this is the part of the ukulele on the far left (the thin end!). One end of each string is fastened to this part of the ukulele. This is where you will find the four 'machine heads' or tuning pegs.

The Machine Heads & Tuning Pegs
'Machine heads' are the little metal and plastic devices located on the headstock of most modern ukuleles. Some older or more traditional ukuleles have plastic and metal or wooden 'tuning pegs' instead of machine heads. Whether you have machine heads or pegs, these are used to tune your ukulele. When you turn them round one way they increase the tension of the strings (turn them round the other way and they decrease the tension). There are four of these (one for each string). The pros and cons of these different tuning devices are explored in the next chapter (see 'Choosing a Ukulele')

The Neck
This is the long, thin part of the ukulele to which the headstock is connected. It's the part of the ukulele where you'll use the fingers on your left hand to hold down strings to play notes and chords.

- The Main Parts of a Ukulele -

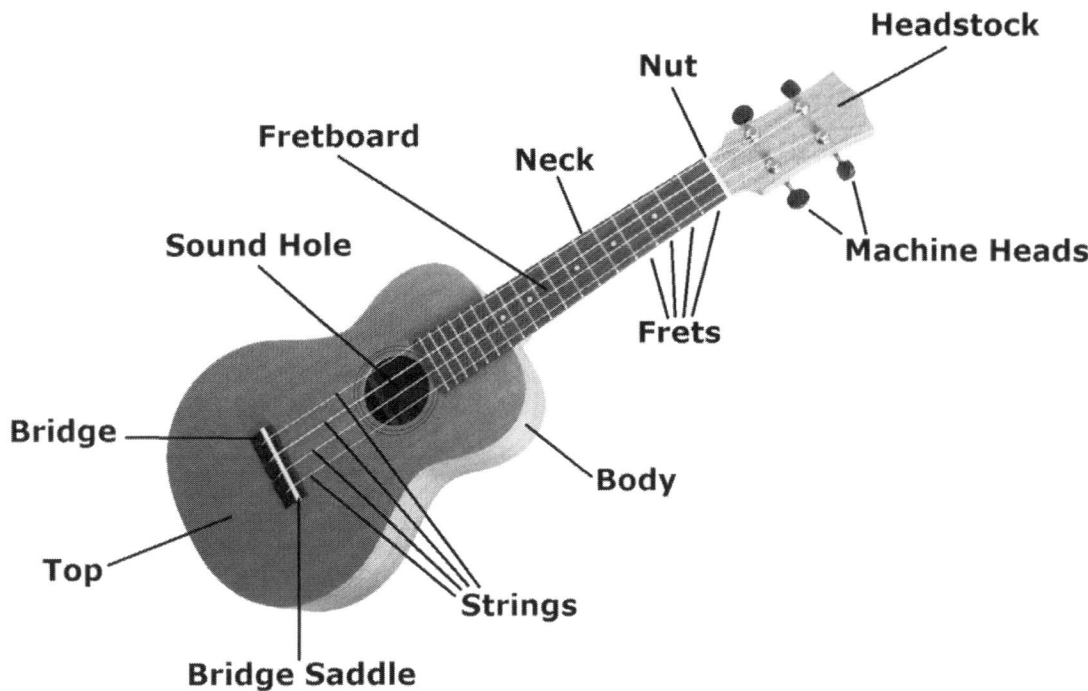

The Nut (sometimes called 'top-nut')
This is the little bit of hard plastic (sometimes bone) that is found at the place where the headstock meets the neck. It has four, small grooves in it, and these are there to hold the strings in place and at the right height.

The Frets
These are created by the thin strips of metal that are located at intervals all the way along the neck of the ukulele. They are referred to as the 1st fret, 2nd fret, 3rd fret, and so on. The 1st fret is the one just next to the nut, the 2nd is the one after that, and so on. Most of the chords and stuff you will be playing to start off with will be played on the 1st, 2nd and 3rd frets.

The Fretboard (sometimes called 'fingerboard')
This is the flat part of the neck where you'll find the frets, and where you hold down (finger) strings to play notes and chords. This is usually made of a harder wood than the rest of the ukulele. It has to be hard, as it gets lots of wear and tear when the ukulele is played.

The Body
This the fattest part of the ukulele to which the neck is connected and the other end of each string is fastened. It's the part of the ukulele that makes the sound (along with the strings, of course).

The body of a ukulele usually has a 'waist' (where it is thinner in the middle than at each end), so that it's easier to hold on your knee when played sitting down. In this way, the ukulele resembles a small acoustic or classical guitar. Some traditional ukes have 'pineapple' shaped bodies, and nowadays you can buy ukuleles that have other weird and wacky shapes too (such as the 'flying V' or heart-shaped ukulele).

- The Main Parts of a Ukulele -

The part of the body of a ukulele that faces away from you when playing is called the 'top' – this is the part that resonates when you play a note. The part of the ukulele that you hold against your body when playing is called the 'back'.

The Sound Hole
This is the round (well, usually) hole in the middle of the body (the top) of the ukulele. Most of the sound a ukulele makes comes out of this hole.

The Bridge
This is the part of the ukulele to which the other end of each string is fastened. It is usually mostly black, and has a thin, white strip of hard plastic (or bone) over which the strings pass. This white strip is called the 'bridge saddle'.

Marilyn Monroe demonstrates an unconventional playing position!

4. Choosing a Ukulele

This section is really aimed at those of you who are keen to learn the ukulele, but do not already possess one. If you already have a uke, then what I have to say may depress you ...or cheer you up.

When buying a new ukulele you're faced with a bit of dilemma: you don't want to spend too much money in case you don't actually take to it like you thought you might (as if!), and you don't want to spend too little money in case you get a poor quality instrument that hinders your ability to learn, or detracts from the enjoyment of playing. For what it's worth, here's my take on this:

Whilst there are some exceptions, you generally get what you pay for. Unless you have money to burn, however, I wouldn't recommend buying the most expensive ukulele you can find. At the time of writing (2013), the price of a new ukulele in the UK varies from around £15 to around £500. There are some very good starter instruments in the £60 to £100 range, and this is what I'd recommend most ukulele beginners pay for their instrument. However, I've tried out some ukuleles in the £200 to £250 range which compare very favourably with those approaching £500. So if you you're feeling that little bit more flush, and you're pretty confident the uke is your destiny, then this may be the range to go for. As I suggested in the introduction, the fact remains that for the price of a pretty mediocre acoustic guitar you can buy a really excellent ukulele.

What makes a good ukulele?

1) Tone
Ukuleles can vary in tone quite markedly. At one end of the spectrum, they can have a rich, 'rounded', ringing tone, such that notes almost resemble those played on a classical guitar; at the other end, they can have a bright, 'twangy' tone. Try a few different ukes out, compare how they sound, and decide which you like the best. Determining which instrument has the better tone can be a very personal judgement.

The tone and volume (i.e., loudness) of a uke are determined by a number of factors, but mainly: the type and quality of wood from which the top and body of the uke is constructed, and the shape and size of the instrument.

Nowadays, lots of different types of wood are used to make the tops and bodies of ukuleles. Traditionally, ukuleles were made from a wood called 'koa'. Koa ukuleles generally sound a little brighter than, for example, mahogany ukuleles, which tend to have a mellower tone. The more expensive ukuleles are made from solid wood, whilst the less expensive ones may be made from laminate. Generally speaking, solid wood will sound better than laminate.

Unusually shaped ukuleles (e.g., the 'flying V' and the heart-shaped uke) can look great and be fun to play, but tend not to sound as good as the traditional, guitar-shaped uke. Ukuleles also come in a variety of different sizes, and these are discussed below.

- Choosing a Ukulele -

2) How well does it tune?
For me, this is one of the most important characteristics of a ukulele. A ukulele with a great tone isn't much use if you can't get it in tune or keep it in tune, and a ukulele with an average tone is still great, if it tunes well.

Many of the cheaper ukuleles have low quality components, and are generally not constructed very well. Without getting into too much technical detail, these not only affect how good a ukulele sounds, but also how well it tunes. With some ukuleles you can get the strings perfectly in tune, but as soon as you play a chord, it sounds out of tune. This can be because the instrument has high 'action', poor 'intonation' or low quality strings (see below).

Traditional and older ukuleles often had tuning pegs which rely on friction to keep the instrument in tune. There are two types: (1) simple,wooden pegs that fit tightly into holes; and (2) plastic and metal pegs that have a screw for tightening. Whilst these can be seen on some modern ukes, most have geared machine heads much like those found on guitars (see pictures below).

Wooden friction tuning pegs

Plastic and metal friction tuning pegs

Geared machine heads

Friction tuning pegs can be a little temperamental, and making very fine adjustments to tuning with wooden pegs can be tricky. The geared machine heads are more reliable, and so, I'd definitely recommend getting an instrument fitted with these. They can have exposed gearing (as in the picture above) or the gearing may be hidden inside sealed units.

If you're a beginner and trying out ukuleles with a view to purchasing one, then how well the instrument tunes may be difficult to establish. From my experience, the staff in musical instrument shops will be honest with you, and if they have someone who knows about ukuleles, they'll give reliable advice and guidance. However, if you know someone who is already reasonably proficient on the uke, I suggest you drag them along to the shop with you.

2) Action
The term 'action' refers to the distance between the strings and the fretboard – it's how far you have to press down the strings to play notes (see picture on right). If your uke has a high action, then your fingers have to work harder, and this will affect how easy it is to learn to play. A high action can also affect tuning, as when you press a string down to the fretboard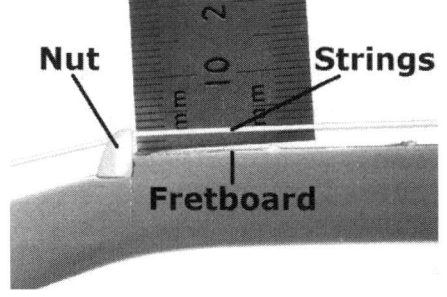

you stretch it a little bit, and this raises the pitch of the note being played. If the action is too low, then strings will vibrate against frets instead of making clear, ringing notes (this is known as 'fret buzz').

A poor action is usually only a problem on some cheaper ukes, and even then, it can often be adjusted. Action is determined by three things: (1) the height of the bridge or bridge saddle; (2) the depths of the grooves in the nut; and (3) the angle of the neck in relation to the body of the uke. (1) and (2) can usually be adjusted (ideally by a musical instrument repairer). Whilst correcting (3) is pretty straight-forward on many guitars, on a ukulele this is fixed (unless you're a skilled luthier, perhaps).

4) Intonation
Without getting too technical, when ukulele players talk about 'intonation' they're referring to how well a uke keeps its tuning as you play notes all the way from the bottom of the fretboard (near the headstock) to the top (near the sound hole). On a good ukulele the notes you play on the higher frets should be in tune with those played when you just pluck a string (without pressing it down onto the fretboard). On some poor ukuleles this isn't the case. This means that even if you get the four strings perfectly in tune, the instrument sounds out of tune when you play notes on the fretboard ...and this will tend to get worse as notes are played higher up the fretboard.

Checking the intonation on a ukulele may be difficult if you're not an experienced musician. So, as suggested above, if you know someone who is already reasonably proficient on the uke (or on the guitar, where the same idea of intonation is important), then drag them along to the shop with you. Generally speaking though, intonation is only a problem on some cheaper ukuleles.

5) Strings
Good quality strings sound better than cheaper ones, stay in tune better, and last longer. Nowadays, most decent quality ukuleles (in the £60 and upwards range) come with good quality strings fitted, and if they don't, a new set of good quality strings won't break the bank (around £6 to £7). 'Aquila' and 'Martin' produce some of the best strings.

What Size of Ukulele Should I Buy?
Ukuleles are made in four main sizes:

The soprano (21") is the smallest in the uke family, and is generally considered the 'standard' ukulele. It has a distinctive, fairly thin, and comparatively quiet, jingly sound. Because it's so small, it's ideal for travelling. They tend to be the cheapest ukuleles too. However, if you're coming to the ukulele from the guitar, or you have pretty chunky fingers (like me!), then you may struggle a little

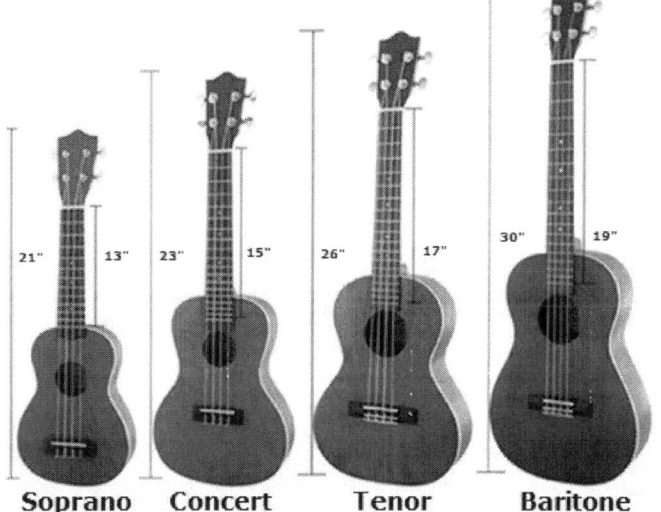

Soprano   Concert   Tenor   Baritone

with the soprano.

The concert (23") is slightly larger than the soprano. The fingerboard is wider and the frets are slightly more spaced out, which can make it a little easier to play than the soprano (if you have fat fingers!). The body is also larger, which means that it makes a slightly richer tone than the soprano, and can also be louder. These have become very popular in recent times, such that the concert uke may soon be the new 'standard'.

The tenor (26") is just a little larger than the concert. It may not feel that different to play than the concert, but because of its larger body, it can have a slightly richer tone. Some players like to tune these to a lower pitch so that the sound resembles that of a guitar.

The baritone (30") is the largest member of the uke family. It is tuned down lower than its relations and has a larger body, both of which help it to sound quite like a guitar. It can be played in much the same way as the smaller ukes, but lacks the bright, crisp sound that can be achieved with the soprano and concert sizes.

Left-Handed?
To play ukulele left-handed, you simply need to swap the strings around on your instrument so that: the 1st (A) is in the position of the 4th (G): the 2nd (E) is in the position of the 3rd (C): and so on. Re-stringing a ukulele isn't too difficult, and there are useful online guides that will help you with this. However, you may prefer to 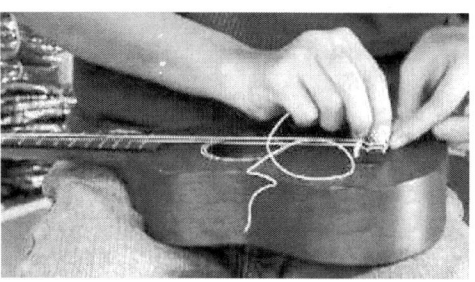 ask someone with experience to do this for you (e.g., someone in a music shop).

Right handed ukuleles with cutaways (such as the one in the picture below) will look a bit odd when played upside down, so it's probably best not to buy one of these. Left-handed ukuleles with cutaways on the other side do exist, but they're not as easy to get hold of as right-handed ones.

Other Considerations
After the above, there aren't really any other major considerations when buying your first ukulele, other than:
- Does the uke feel good to play?
- Does the uke look good to you?

Nevertheless, you may wish to consider the following:

Ukuleles with Cutaways (with a section missing on one side where the neck meets the body) can look really cool (see picture on right). The cutaway is there to make accessing the frets at the top of the fingerboard easier. However, for most players this is almost  never an issue, as they tend to play pretty much everything at the other end of the fingerboard (and venture into the middle on rare occasions). The sound of the uke doesn't seem to be affected by the cutaway though, so if you like the look of it...

Electro-Acoustic Ukuleles have pickups built into them (and sometimes tone, volume and tuning controls too) that allow you to plug the instrument into an amplifier or PA system. This is really useful if you wish to perform at open mike nights, folk clubs, gigs, etc. The best electro-acoustic ukes sound pretty much as good amplified as they do acoustically (and vice versa!).

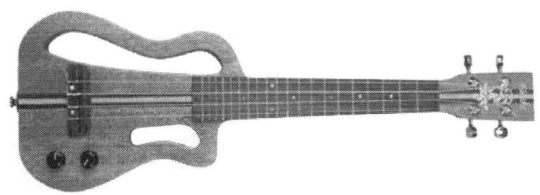

Electric Ukuleles are solid bodied instruments that can be plugged into an amplifier or PA system, as with an electro-acoustic. They tend to have volume and tone controls built in. The amplified sound of these may be less like an acoustic instrument than an amplified electro-acoustic uke. As the sound is taken directly from the strings by pickups, the shape of the instrument isn't important. Hence, these can be made in a variety of different strange and interesting shapes, and can even have holes right through them (as in the picture above).

When not plugged in, electric ukuleles make very little noise, which can be an advantage if you want to practice without disturbing anyone else (my girlfriend uses one for practicing when staying in hotels), but otherwise can limit how much use you'll get out of it. Hence, I wouldn't recommend getting an electric uke as a first instrument.

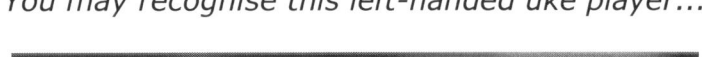

You may recognise this left-handed uke player...

5. Playing Positions

Before you can begin to play the ukulele, you really need to know how to hold it and where to position your left hand. These are called 'playing positions'.

Holding Your Ukulele

When it comes to holding your ukulele in order to play, there are four main options:

1. Rest the body of the ukulele on your right leg or in your lap whilst in a seated position (see picture on right). With this option you may also apply a little pressure with you right forearm to hold the ukulele against your tummy, and use your left hand to support the ukulele at an angle so that the headstock is slightly higher than the body;

2. Rest the body of the ukulele (i.e., the 'waist', if you have a standard shaped instrument) on your left leg whilst in a seated position. With this option you may need to apply a little pressure with you right forearm to hold the ukulele against your tummy and at an angle so that the headstock is slightly higher than the body (see picture on left). The ukulele will be fully supported, so that your left hand can move freely around the neck and fretboard;

3. Use a strap (that goes around your neck or back) to suspend the ukulele against your chest or tummy (see pictures on right). This can be done either in a seated position or when standing. The ukulele will be fully supported, so that your left hand can move freely around the neck and fretboard. Straps for ukuleles can be purchased at most good musical instrument shops;

4. Hold the ukulele against your chest by supporting it with your right forearm and left hand (see picture on right). This can be done either in a seated position or when standing. Ukuleles are usually pretty light, and so, supporting the instrument without a strap like this is manageable with a little practice. You

- 20 -

may find this option a little tricky to begin with though, as it can be hard to play certain chord shapes and to change between chords when, to some extent, you're also relying on your left hand to support the ukulele.

Ultimately, whether you sit down on a chair, stand up, use a strap, sit cross-legged on the floor, or jump up and down whilst you're playing ...that's up to you. Do what feels most comfortable and makes it easy for you to play whilst you're learning.

Left Hand Playing Positions
Now let's consider how you position your left hand. A classical guitar teacher will tell you to place the top part of your thumb on the back of the neck so that it looks like the thumb in the picture below. Some ukulele players also adopt this playing position.

Placing the top part of your thumb on the back of the neck in this way allows you to bring the fingers of your left hand round onto the fingerboard, which in turn, enables you to finger notes easily. However, many ukulele players usually don't do this when playing open chords (I usually don't). Instead, they position the left hand so that the thumb sticks out over the top of the fretboard (see picture below).

Positioning my hand like this when playing open chords doesn't affect how easily I can play. In fact, I find it necessary to have my hand in this position if I want to play standing up without a strap, as this allows me to support the neck of the instrument a little (see 'Holding Your Ukulele') – try this out and you should see what I mean.

My recommendation would be that you should do whatever suits you. Provided you can play nice, clear notes and chords, then it doesn't really matter! Just try to play as well as you can, and if you're having trouble making notes ring out clearly, then try swivelling your hand around the neck, one way or another, and see if this helps.

6. Tuning Your Ukulele

Getting your ukulele in tune can mean two things: 1) making sure all of the strings on your ukulele are in tune with each other; and 2) making sure your ukulele is in tune with other instruments (which is important if you're playing with other musicians, but not important if you're not). When the strings aren't in tune with each other, your ukulele will sound pretty horrible. If you're playing your ukulele along with other instruments, the music you make will sound pretty horrible if you are out of tune with them.

There are various ways to do this, but I'm going to describe to you the one I tend to use for the standard ukulele tuning (G C E A – sometimes called 'C tuning'). Here goes:

1) Tuning the C string
First of all you should tune the C (or 3rd) string. This is the lowest pitched of the four strings. To do this you will need to get this note from somewhere else, such as another musical instrument which is already in tune (e.g., a piano or keyboard) or from pitch pipes (a small device which you blow to make the correct note, and which sounds a bit like a harmonica). On the right is a picture showing where to find a 'middle C' on a piano or keyboard.

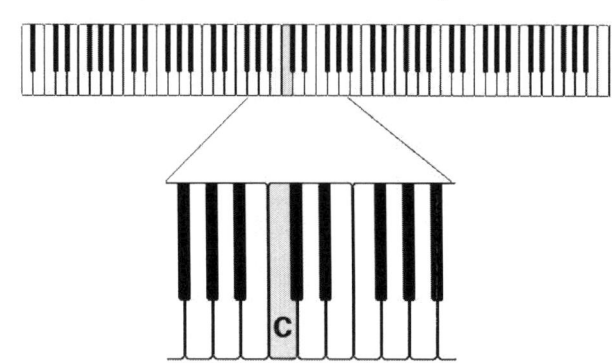

The note you already have on your C string may be higher or lower in pitch than the note it should be. Of course, you may be very lucky, and find that your C string already has the right note! Here's what you do if it hasn't though:
  i. Play the correct C note on the other instrument or device;
  ii. Gently pluck the C string on your ukulele with your thumb;
  iii. Listen very carefully and decide if the note on your ukulele is higher or lower than the correct note;
  iv. Turn the machine head for the C string either clockwise or anti-clockwise a small amount, depending on whether you wish to raise or lower the pitch of the string;
  v. Repeat i. to iv. until your ukulele's C string has the same note as the other instrument or device.

2) Tuning the E string
  i. Using the index finger (1st finger) on your left hand, press down the C string of your ukulele on the **4th fret**, and then gently pluck the string. This note will be an E;
  ii. Gently pluck your E (or 2nd) string;
  iii. Decide if the note on your E string is higher or lower than the correct note (as played on the C string);
  iv. Turn the machine head for the E string either clockwise or anti-clockwise a small amount;

- Tuning Your Ukulele -

    v.   Repeat i. to iv. until your ukulele's E string has the same note as the E note you have played on your C string.

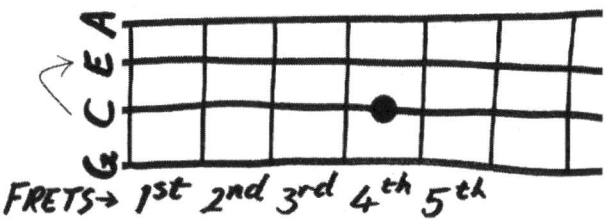

3) Tuning the A string

The procedure here is more-or-less the same as I've described above when tuning the E string. This time, using the index finger on your left hand, press down the E string of your ukulele on the **5th fret**, and then gently pluck the string. This note will be an A. Compare this note with the note on your A (or 1st) string and adjust the note on this string as you have already done with the C and E strings.

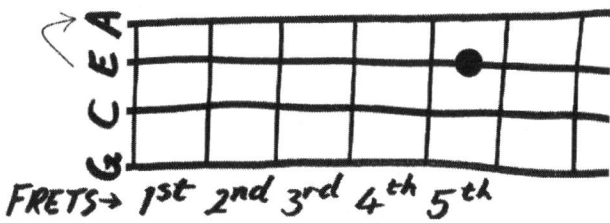

4) Tuning the G string

This time, you press down the E string on the **3rd fret**, and then gently pluck the string. This note will be a G. Compare this note with the note on your G (or 4th) string and adjust the note on this string as you have already done with the C, E and A strings.

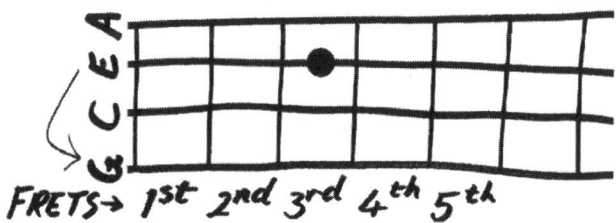

Some Final Thoughts

As with most things you do on your ukulele, the more you practice this procedure, the better you'll get at it. The more experienced you get on the ukulele, the more sensitive your ears will get to differences between notes when tuning it. Very experienced musicians can hear very tiny differences between notes, and so, can be much pickier about tuning their instruments. Whereas, when you're new to this, you may not be able to hear when your ukulele is slightly out of tune.

- Tuning Your Ukulele -

Nowadays, lots of people use electronic tuners to tune their ukuleles. These are definitely very useful devices. They're easy to use and they aren't always very expensive (upwards of about £8). If you use an electronic ukulele tuner you can usually get your ukulele perfectly in tune, which is why lots of learners rely on these. However, you may not always have one of these handy or you may just want to check your tuning very quickly, so you should definitely know how to tune your ukulele yourself too.

You'll probably need to tune your ukulele, at least a little bit, before each playing session and after playing it for a little while.

Ukuleles can go out of tune for a number of reasons:
1) Extreme temperature changes can cause ukulele strings to expand and contract, and so, change their notes. Hence, if you take your ukulele outside on a cold day after it has been tuned in a warm house, it may go out of tune;
2) Just picking/plucking, strumming or fretting notes can eventually pull your strings a little bit out of tune;
3) Accidentally knocking the machine heads (e.g., when leaning you ukulele against a wall, laying it down on the floor, or putting it into a ukulele case) can de-tune your instrument. So, to avoid having to do too much re-tuning, try to be careful how and where you leave your ukulele when you're not playing it;
4) Very new ukulele strings tend to go out of tune until they've settled in;
5) Very old ukulele strings can lose their ability to stay at the correct tension.

Hula dancing may send your uke out of tune too!

7. A Few Musical Terms Defined

This chapter contains brief definitions of a few musical terms that will allow me to explain (and you to understand) how to play your ukulele. Please forgive me if you know some or all of these terms already. It's important that you have a clear grasp of the concepts that are defined here before proceeding through the guide. I'll define any other musical terms I use as we go along.

Note
A 'note' is the musical sound that is created when you pluck a string on your ukulele. These are given the alphabetical labels: A B C D E F and G.

Pitch
The word 'pitch' simply refers to how high or low a note is. The third string on your ukulele makes a lower note than the first string. Hence, the third string has a lower pitch than the first.

Scale
A 'scale' is simply a series of notes that go together well and that are used together to play tunes. There are various different types of scale. When I mention scales in this guide, I'll be referring to 'major scales'. These are the most common types of scale (in western culture).

Scales are labelled according to the first note that appears in the scale when the notes are arranged in ascending order of pitch. The C major scale is shown on the right.

There are seven different notes in a major scale. After the seventh note, the notes repeat themselves but have a higher pitch than those preceding them (notice how the eighth note in the scale, like the first, is a C).

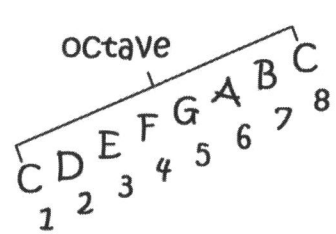

Octave
The term 'octave' refers to the eight note separation between two notes with the same name. For example, the two C notes in the picture on the left are an octave apart.

If you sing the first line in the song "Somewhere Over the Rainbow", the "Some-" and the "-where" are sung an octave apart.

Key
The term 'key' refers to the scale that is used to play a particular tune or song. For example, if the notes in a song fit into a G scale, then the song is said to be played in the key of G.

- A Few Musical Terms Defined -

Tones & Semitones

The difference in pitch between any two neighbouring notes in a major scale is either a 'tone' or a 'semitone'. A semitone is half a tone.

In any major scale, the difference in pitch between the third and fourth notes and between the seventh and eighth is always a semitone. All other differences between neighbouring notes are tones. For example, in the C major scale (see previous page) the difference in pitch between E and F and between B and C is one semitone. The difference between C and D and between D and E, etc. is a tone.

Sometimes a tone is called a 'step' and a semitone is called a 'half step'. On the ukulele a tone difference equates to two frets, whilst a semitone difference equates to one fret.

Sharp & Flat

When tuning your ukulele the term 'sharp' can mean 'slightly higher in pitch', and the term 'flat' can mean 'slightly lower in pitch'. For example, the note made by an open string may be sharp or flat relative to the note it's supposed to be (and would therefore, need tuning).

The word 'sharp' is also used to label a note that is a semitone higher in pitch than another note. In musical notation, the symbol '#' means sharp. Hence, C# ('C sharp') is one semitone higher than C.

If these girls can do it, so can you!

The word 'flat' is also used to label a note that is a semitone lower in pitch than another note. In musical notation, the symbol 'b' means flat. Hence, Db ('D flat') is one semitone lower than D. A Db sounds the same as a C# (these are just different ways of labelling the same note).

Here are all of the notes that can be played on a ukulele, arranged in ascending order of pitch (left to right):

1	2	3	4	5	6	7	8	9	10	11	12
C	C# or Db	D	D# or Eb	E	F	F# or Gb	G	G# or Ab	A	A# or Bb	B

As you can see, there are twelve different notes, and there are no sharps or flats between E and F and between B and C (as they are one semitone apart).

As for why notes are labelled like this ...well, that's partly down to logic, partly, history and partly cultural ...don't blame me!

8. First Chords

A chord is what you hear when at least three different notes are played on different strings of a ukulele, all at the same time. Many great folk, blues, country, pop and rock songs can be played with as few as three chords, so don't worry about learning hundreds of these straight away.

'Open' Chords

If you strum your ukulele without pressing any strings onto the fretboard with your left hand, then you're playing four 'open' strings. 'Open' chords are chords that contain one or more of these open strings, and they tend to be played on the first three frets of your fretboard. Open chords are very useful. In fact, many ukulele players only ever use open chords.

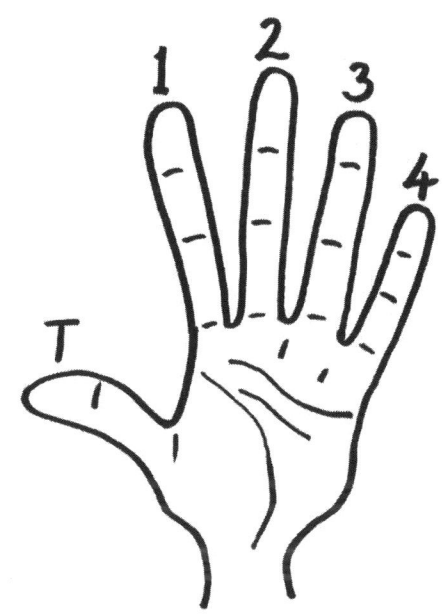

Before I introduce you to chord diagrams so that you can learn some chords, it's useful to assign numbers to the fingers on your left hand.

As you can see from the picture on the left, your index finger is your 1st finger, your middle finger is your 2nd finger, your ring finger is your 3rd finger, and your little finger is your 4th finger.

(American's sometimes refer to the little finger as the 'pinky' – you may come across this if you look at instructional videos online that were made in the U.S.A).

If you have long fingernails on your left hand, then I'm afraid you're going to have to cut them. Long fingernails can get in the way when you're trying to press strings down onto the fretboard. If you're not sure how short to cut them, have a look at the ends of my fingers in the photographs on the next page.

So, now we can look at some chord diagrams. The chord diagrams for three very useful, and commonly used chords, are shown below.

Each diagram shows the four strings of the ukulele and the first three frets of the fretboard (as if you're looking at the fretboard face on, and your ukulele is standing upright). The dots show where you should place your fingers, and the numbers at the top of the diagrams show which finger should be used and which strings should be left open (indicated by a '0'). Not all chord

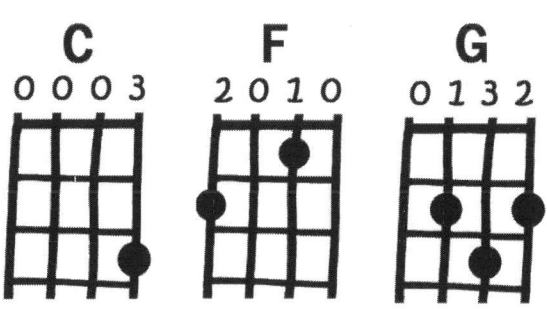

diagrams that you'll come across indicate which fingers you should use like this, but I thought this would help you in getting to grips with your first chords.

- First Chords -

The photographs below show what your hand should look like when playing each of these chords. Try to make your hand look like mine.

C   F   G

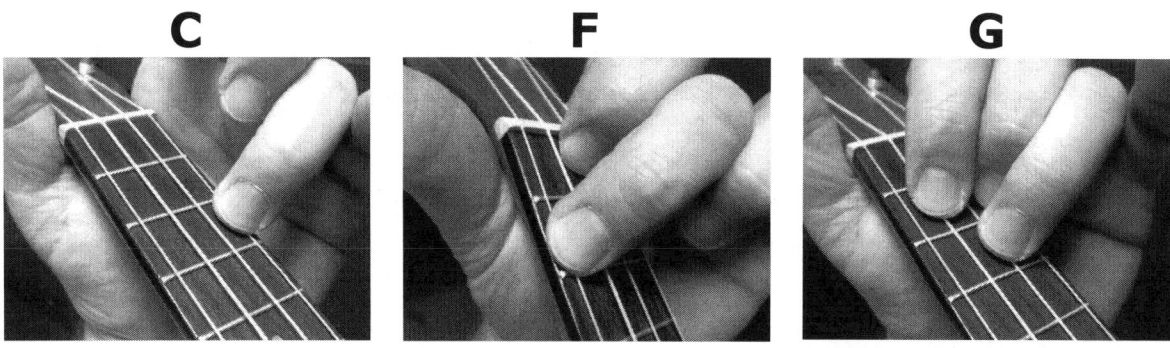

Now have a go at playing each chord. You should find the C chord pretty easy to play, whilst the F and the G may be a little more challenging, at least at first. Try to press down the strings with the fleshy parts of your fingers, right at the end, just behind your fingernails. Then, for each chord, strum the strings slowly and gently downwards (from the 4th to the 1st string) with the tip of the thumb of your right hand. Hold your thumb at an angle of approximately 20° to 45° to the strings

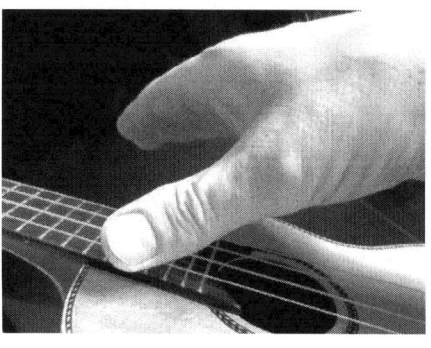

(see picture on right), and try to keep your thumb fairly limp or floppy. This is called a 'down-strum'.

How do the chords sound? If you're fingering the chords well, then the four strings you have strummed should make a nice, clear sound. This is probably true for the C, since you're only using one finger with this chord. However, as these are your first attempts, it's possible that only some of the strings sound clear with the F and the G chord – one or two of the strings may just make dull thuds or buzzing noises. The thuds or buzzes have three main causes:
   1) you're not holding down the fretted strings hard enough;
   2) a finger is not positioned correctly on a fret;
   3) a finger that is fretting one string is also touching another, and stopping it ringing out.

Causes 1) and 2) are easy to address. First, try applying a little more pressure when holding down the strings. This may be tricky, and can make your fingers ache at first. With practice however, your fingers will get stronger and more used to doing this.

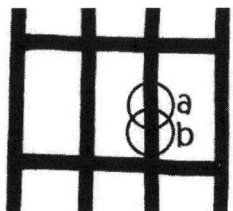

Second, check that your fingers are holding down the strings somewhere in between the middle of a fret and just behind the fret-wire (the metal bit) that makes the note. That is, somewhere between a and b in the diagram to the left.

- First Chords -

Cause 3) can be addressed by having a closer look at your fingers and what they're doing when you play a chord. Each of your fingers has three man parts:
1) the part where you would normally wear a ring;
2) the middle part;
3) the end part, where you have fingernails, and that is used to press down strings.

You should try to position your fingers so that the end parts are approaching a right-angle to the fretboard, as shown in the picture below.

If you were able to look from the direction of your ukulele's headstock, then this is what your fingers should look like when playing an F chord. The two black dots represent the two open strings in this chord. Notice how the angle of the fingers means that these strings are left untouched.

Cause 3) can also be addressed by paying some attention to how you position your left hand, and, how you hold your ukulele (see 'Playing Positions').

Now have another go at strumming each of these chords in turn, starting with the C. Slowly and gently strum downwards with your thumb, as you did earlier. When you've strummed the C eight times (count aloud to yourself, or in your head if you prefer), then change, as smoothly as you can, to the F. Slowly strum this chord eight times, before changing, as smoothly as you can, to the G. Repeat this exercise round and round a few times until you start to feel the chord changes getting a little easier and smoother. Try to make each chord sound as clear as you can make it. Don't worry about trying any fancy strumming just yet.

Don't get frustrated if your playing isn't sounding very good yet – with practice, it will! Changing between chords can be pretty tricky at first, and it may take a bit of time and effort getting your fingers into the right positions each time you move from one chord to another. With practice, however, this will become easier and smoother, so that eventually it will seem almost effortless.

Some Final Thoughts
When you're first learning to play the ukulele you'll probably get sore fingers on your left hand. Eventually, if you practice often enough and for long enough, the ends of these fingers will become calloused (a bit like the skin on the heel of your foot), so that they no longer get sore when you play.

If you really want to learn, then you'll need to practice. I would suggest that you practice for at least half an hour each day. Run through each of the exercises presented in this guide over and over until what you're doing begins to feel reasonably easy, and you're starting to make some good sounds.

Of course, when you learn more and start to make better and better sounds, you may want to practice much more than half an hour a day. In fact, you'll probably find that it doesn't seem like practice at all, but just fun.

9. Chord Progressions and a First Song

A 'chord progression' is simply a series of chords that are played together in a set order (e.g., when accompanying yourself, or someone else, singing a song). So far, you've learned the chords C, F and G. These are the main three chords that you use when you want to play in the key of C (which is a very popular ukulele key).

When your chords are starting to sound reasonably clear, have a go at playing the simple chord progression presented below. In the notation used, each forward slash represents a beat. For now, make gentle down-strums with the thumb of your right hand on each beat – this is actually a very effective and popular strumming pattern and technique. Try to make contact with the strings just over the place where the fretboard meets the body of your ukulele. I have grouped the beats into groups of four – in this chord progression, each group of four beats is a 'bar', and the bold slashes indicate the first beat in a bar.

A Chord Progression in the Key of C:

```
C                                               F
/ / / /   / / / /   / / / /   / / / /   / / / /   / / / /
C                   G         F         C
/ / / /   / / / /   / / / /   / / / /   / / / /   / / / /
```

Most music you will play on the ukulele will have four-beat bars like this. When learning some new pieces of music it can sometimes be useful to count along with the beats as you're playing – this can help you to keep track of what you're doing. With this chord progression you might find it handy to count: **one**, *two, three, four,* **one**, *two, three, four* ...and so on (accent the 'one' as this indicates the start of each bar). There are twelve bars in this chord progression.

When you play music with four-beat bars like this, you are said to be playing in '4/4 timing' ('four-four timing') - the first 4 indicates how many beats there are in a bar (don't worry about what the second 4 means ...I never do!). Most rock, pop, folk and blues music, etc. has 4/4 timing. Another popular time signature (that's what these '4/4' things are called) is 3/4 ('three-four'). Here, there are three beats in every bar. This 3/4 timing is sometimes called 'waltz timing'.

Anyway, back to the chord progression: Start off strumming very slowly, and try your best to keep a steady beat (without speeding up or slowing down). If you strum slowly enough, you'll allow yourself time to change chords without upsetting the steady beat. When you get to the end of the progression, go right back to the beginning without missing a beat, and start it all over again. Keep doing this until it starts to feel easier (or until your hands get too tired!).

As playing this progression starts to feel easier and begins to sound better, try speeding up your playing a little.

In case you hadn't yet guessed, this is a simple 'twelve-bar blues' chord progression, and could be used to accompany lots of different songs (e.g., Elvis Presley's 'Blue Suede Shoes' & 'Hound Dog'; Billy Haley & the Comets' 'Shake

- Chord Progressions and a First Song -

Rattle & Roll' & 'Rock Around the Clock'; Chuck Berry's 'Johnny B. Goode' & 'Roll Over Beethoven'). In fact, loads of rock 'n' roll and blues songs use twelve bar blues chord progressions, as well as the occasional modern pop and rock song.

Twelve-Bar Blues – in the Key of G
The chord progression I introduced earlier is in the key of C, and the three main chords in the key of C are C, F and G. Below are the three main chords that are used in the key of G.

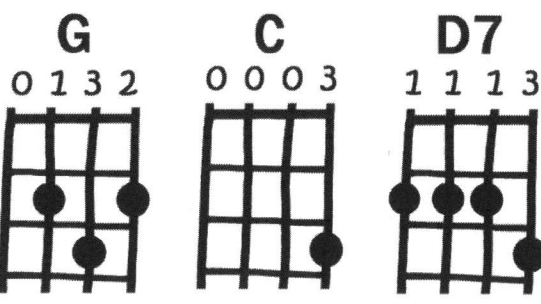

Of course, you've already come across the G and the C chord. To play the D7 chord you need to place your first finger across all four strings on the second fret, and then hold down the first string on the third fret using your third finger (or your second finger, if you prefer). With this chord you're 'barring' the top four strings with your index finger (in ukulele/guitar jargon, 'to bar' means to hold down several strings with one finger).

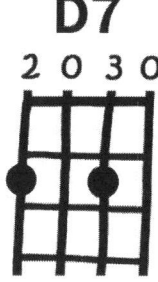

The barred fingering of a D7 chord is the one you'll see in most ukulele chord books and charts. However, many beginners struggle to bar strings like this. Whilst it's worth persevering (barring is a useful technique to develop), if you're having a lot of difficulty, then you may wish to use the alternative D7 fingering shown on the right.

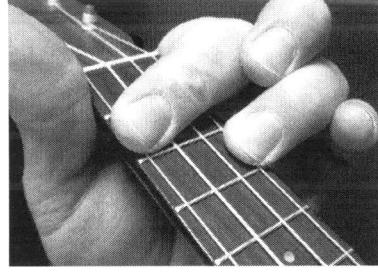 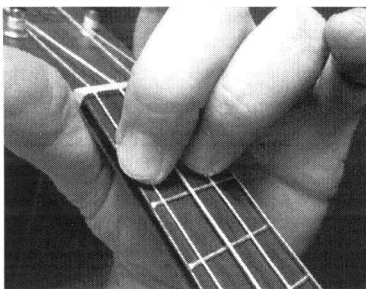

With the barred D7 fingering each string produces a different note. Hence, it perhaps has a fuller sound than the non-barred version, with which the same note is made on the first and fourth strings. Personally, I use both versions in different situations: in up tempo songs that also have rapid chord changes, I find that using the non-barred version allows me to play more smoothly; and in some songs, one version just seems to sound better than the other.

Anyway, back to the chord progression: you may find that you would like to play a song with a twelve-bar blues progression, but playing the song in the key of C doesn't suit your voice (because it means that you have to strain to sing really high, or struggle to sing down low). Well, with these chords you can be play the same twelve-bar blues chord progression you've already come across, but in the key of G. Chances are that if playing a song in C doesn't suit your voice, then it'll be just about right in the key of G. Here's what the chord progression looks like in G:

A Twelve-Bar Blues Chord Progression in the Key of G:

```
G                                           C
/ / / /   / / / /   / / / /   / / / /   / / / /   / / / /
G                       D7          C           G
/ / / /   / / / /   / / / /   / / / /   / / / /   / / / /
```

Changing the key of a song or chord progression like this is called 'transposition'. I often have to transpose songs from the key in which they were originally played on famous recordings to one that suits my singing range.

To illustrate the use of this chord progression I've presented the lyrics and chords to Elvis Presley's 'Hound Dog' (arranged in the key of C) on the next page.

This is a pretty simple song with just two verses which are repeated, plus solos (have a listen to the record to get the full arrangement). As before, each forward slash represents a beat – make gentle down-strums with the thumb of your right hand on each beat. Exclamation marks are used to indicate short, sharp strums, after which there is silence until the next chord is indicated (you should stop these chords from ringing by gently placing the palm of your hand across the four strings).

Elvis demonstrating his favourite uke chord with two, star struck ladies!

- Chord Progressions and a First Song -

Hound Dog (Lieber/Stoller)

```
                        C  /   /   /  / /
You ain't nothin' but a hound dog
  /    /     /   / / /
Cryin' all the time
/      / /        /     F  /   /   /  / /
  You ain't nothin' but a hound dog
  /    /    C  / / /
Cryin' all the time
 /  /  /    /  G    /       /
  Well,  you ain't never caught a rabbit
  /    F  /    /   /  C  / / / C!
And you ain't no friend of mine


                        C  /   /   /
When they said you was high  classed
/  /    /    /    /     / / /
  Well, that was just a lie
/  /    /       / F  /   /   /
  Yeah, they said you was high  classed
/  /    /    /    /     / / /
  Well, that was just a lie
/  /  /    /  G    /       /
  Yeah,  you ain't never caught a rabbit
  /    F  /    /   /  C  / / / C!
And you ain't no friend of mine
```

- 33 -

10. Strumming Techniques

So far, you've been playing down-strums on your ukulele with your thumb. Whilst this can be a very useful strumming technique, you've probably noticed that this isn't how every player strums all of the time. When you first start to play the ukulele, or when you learn a new song, you'll need to consider which method(s) of strumming you're going to use: (1) thumb; (2) index finger; or (3) pick/plectrum.

Personally, I almost always strum using my index finger, as I find this to be the most versatile technique. Indeed, I think this is the most common strumming method. Occasionally, however, I use my thumb to make a softer sound in certain songs, and sometimes use my index finger *and* thumb to play certain 'special' strums (e.g., the 'triple strum'). Whilst I always use a pick to strum when playing a steel string guitar, I've never really got on with using a pick to strum the ukulele, as I can't achieve the sound or maintain the level of control I want. Nevertheless, some very good players prefer to strum with the thumb or with a pick.

Whichever method you decide to use, I would recommend that you:
- strum the strings more-or-less over the end of the fretboard. You *can* strum over the body or sound hole too (as is usual on a guitar), but I find this makes the uke sound a little too bright and harsh;
- try to move your hand by swivelling from the wrist, instead of moving your whole forearm from the elbow (this should give you more control of your strumming and a smoother sound).

Have a look at some of the videos that ukulele players have uploaded onto Youtube to see how they strum their instrument on different types of song (have a look at my 'ukulelejez' channel, at: www.youtube.com/ukulelejez). This should give you a good idea of the different sounds that can be achieved and how different strumming methods look in practice.

Here are a few words on each of those strumming methods:

(1) Thumb
Here's how to strum using your thumb:

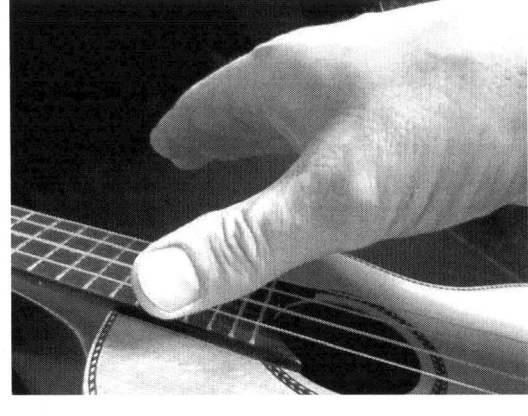

- hold your thumb at an angle of approximately 20° to 45° to the strings;
- try to keep your thumb limp/floppy, so that you can play softly when required (a rigid thumb will usually make a louder sound);
- using the edge of the fleshy part of your thumb, make contact with the strings in a smooth downward motion (from the 4th to the 1st string). This is called a 'down-strum';
- using the edge of the thumbnail, make contact with the strings in a smooth upward motion (from the 1st to the 4th string). This is called an 'up-strum'.

- Strumming Techniques -

(2) Index finger
Here's how to strum using your index finger:

- hold your index finger at an angle of approximately 70° to 90° to the strings;
- try to keep your finger limp/floppy, so that you can play softly when required (a rigid finger will usually make a louder sound);
- keep your thumb out of the way of your index finger (by tucking it in or sticking it out at right angles to the index finger);
- using the edge of the fingernail, make contact with the strings in a smooth downward motion (from the 4th to the 1st string) to play down-strums;
- position your index finger so that the joints in your finger allow it to bend freely with down-strums;
- using the edge of the fleshy part of your finger, make contact with the strings in a smooth upward motion (from the 1st to the 4th string) to play up-strums.

Strumming with the index finger makes a different sound to strumming with the thumb. As I see it, there are three main reasons for this:
1. the index finger is typically thinner than the thumb; therefore, the index finger makes less contact with the strings;
2. the index finger has more joints than the thumb; therefore, the index finger can bend more freely;
3. down-strums with the index finger typically involve using the edge of the fingernail, while up-strums use the fleshy part of the fingertip – the reverse is true with the thumb. This means that down-strums with the index finger typically have a slightly sharper tone than with the thumb, and up-strums have a slightly softer tone with the index finger than with the thumb.

(3) Picks/Plectrums
'Pick' and 'plectrum' are just different words for the same thing. The word 'plectrum' is a more formal or old-fashioned word than 'pick'. Strictly speaking, the correct plural of the word plectrum is not 'plectrums' (as I've typed above), but 'plectra'. However, if you go into a music shop and tell the shop assistant that you wish to buy some 'plectra', they'll probably look very confused, or else, laugh their heads off – so it's probably best just to ask for 'picks'. I'm going to use the word 'pick' from now on ...unless I forget.

Plectrums come in a variety of colours, materials and thicknesses, but they're usually, more-or-less the same shape (like a triangle with the angles rounded off). The picks that ukulele players tend to use are made of a kind of rigid felt material, although you could also use a more standard, plastic pick (ideally, quite a soft/flexible one).

- Strumming Techniques -

It's important to get used to holding your pick correctly, between the thumb and first finger of your right hand, so that the thinnest part of the pick sticks out ready to hit the strings. When looking down at your hand, it should look pretty much like the picture on the right.

Obviously, you'll need to hold your pick tightly enough for it not to fall out of your hand or twist around in your fingers, but not so tightly that you can only make a hard or loud sound. You should try to hit the strings lightly with just the tip the pick.

Formal attire isn't necessary when strumming your uke with a group of friends on a park bench!

11. Six Really Useful Strumming Patterns

Rhythms can be varied on the ukulele by playing different combinations of 'down-strums', 'up-strums', missing the strings all together, and varying how hard you strum. Guitarists and ukulele players call these 'strumming patterns'.

There are many possible strumming patterns, but most players most of the time only use a few different ones when accompanying their singing. This is largely because people tend to specialise in playing particular types of song. I would suggest trying to master three or four patterns for general usage, and then learning other patterns if and when they are needed for new songs you may wish to play. When you feel familiar with how strumming patterns work, you can have a go at creating your own.

The six strumming patterns I'll describe here are the ones that I find most useful and versatile. I'll explain how you can vary these patterns to suit different songs and styles of music you may wish to play. After describing each strumming pattern I'll present a new song for you to have a go at using the pattern. From this point onwards, I won't be using forward slashes to show the beats/down-strums throughout the songs I'll be presenting (as with 'Hound Dog') – if you know a song well enough by ear, you shouldn't need these. There may be a few forward slashes at the ends of verses, however, at points where I think a little timing guidance may be needed.

Strumming Pattern #1
This first strumming pattern I'm going to introduce is perhaps the simplest you can play. In fact, you've already been using it! The pattern simply involves strumming downwards, once on every beat. It sounds great in pretty much any song, so it's a useful fall back option when you're first working your way through a new song. This pattern is especially well suited to old 'music hall'/vaudeville style songs and up-tempo, jazzy songs.

On the next page there's a classic, 1960s protest song from Bob Dylan that sounds great when played using this strumming pattern. It's arranged in the key of C, and so the chords are C and F (which you already know), but on this occasion, instead of G you'll be playing a G7 chord. The chord diagram and fingering for this chord are shown on the right.

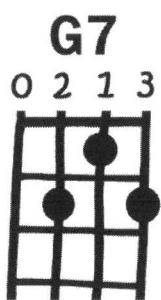 

Here's a little technical tip that can make playing this and similar chord progressions a little easier: if you compare an F with a G7 you'll see that they have one finger and note in common: the first finger on the first fret of the second string. When changing form an F to a G7, therefore, leave this finger where it is and simply lift up your second finger and place this and your third finger in the correct positions. Your fingers will be making a step across the fretboard instead of a jump, enabling you to finger the G7 more smoothly and with less effort.

- Six Really Useful Strumming Patterns -

Blowin' in the Wind (Bob Dylan)

Intro: C / / / / / / /

```
C            F         G7         C
How many roads must a man walk down
              F         C
Before you call him a man?
              F         G7        C
How many seas must a white dove sail
              F         G7
Before she sleeps in the sand?
         C         F         G7         C
Yes and how many times must the cannonballs fly
              F         C    / / /  / / /
Before they're forever banned?

      /   F         G7        C          F
      The answer my friend is blowin' in the wind
                    G7        C    / / /  / / /
      The answer is blowin' in the wind
```

        Break: F / / / G7 / / / C / / / F / / / / / / / G7 / / / C / / / / / / /

Yes, and how many years can a mountain exist
Before it's washed to the sea?
Yes and how many years can some people exist
Before they're allowed to be free?
Yes and how many times can a man turn his head
And pretend that he just doesn't see?

      The answer my friend is blowin' in the wind
      The answer is blowin' in the wind

        Break: F / / / G7 / / / C / / / F / / / / / / / G7 / / / C / / / / / / /

Yes, and how many times must a man look up
Before he can see the sky?
Yes and how many ears must one man have
Before he can hear people cry?
Yes and how many deaths will it take till he knows
That too many people have died?

      The answer my friend is blowin' in the wind
      The answer is blowin' in the wind

Outro: F / / / G7 / / / C / / / F / / / / / / / G7 / / / C / / / /

- Six Really Useful Strumming Patterns -

Strumming Pattern #2
The next strumming pattern I'm going to describe is one that guitarists and uke players use a great deal, and can be used in pretty much any song in 4/4 time (i.e., most pop, rock and folk songs). This pattern is one bar (i.e., four beats) long, and can simply be repeated with every bar of the song you're playing. It sounds great when played with a straight rhythm, or with a bouncy, 'swing' or 'shuffle' rhythm (to suit the rhythm of the song you're playing, of course).

For this strumming pattern you will be moving your strumming hand up and down at a consistent speed. Now, without actually hitting any strings yet, I'd like you to move your hand up and down slowly, near to the strings. As mentioned earlier, try to move your hand by swivelling from the wrist, instead of moving your whole forearm from the elbow. Say "down" to yourself when your hand is moving down, and "up" when your hand is moving up; you should now be saying: "down, up, down, up, down, up, down up, ..." This will probably feel a bit silly, I know, but it will help you to learn the strumming patterns I'm going to describe to you. Try to make sure that each down movement takes the same amount of time as each up movement. I suggest that each movement takes about half a second (so that your hand moves down once every second).

Once you've got your hand moving up and down at a consistent pace, make a C chord with your left hand, and bring your right hand closer to the strings so that you begin gently strumming all the strings of your ukulele up and down. Keep on saying "down, up, down, up, down, up, down up, ..." to yourself. Try to make the down-strums sound as a clear and as loud as the up-strums. When you feel that you're making a nice even sound at a steady pace, you'll be ready to have a go at playing the strumming pattern.

To play the four-beat, strumming pattern, all you need to do is miss the strings sometimes when you move your hand up or down.

Up until now, for every bar, you have been playing:

down, up, down, up, down up, down, up

Each down-strum has been on a beat and each up-strum has been in the space between each beat. This could also be written like this:

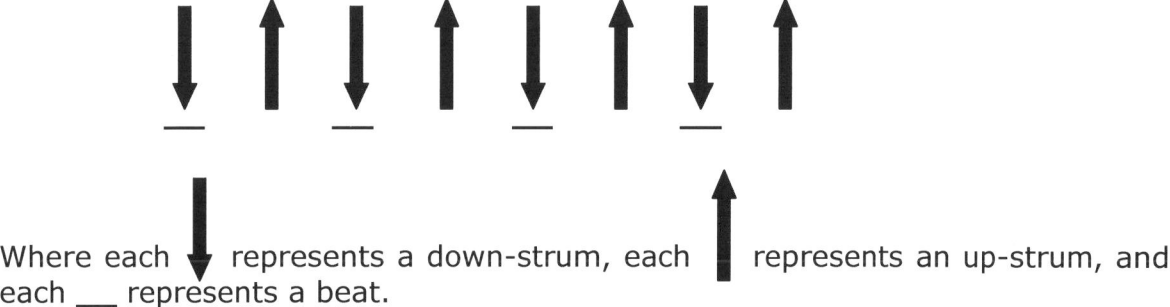

Where each ↓ represents a down-strum, each ↑ represents an up-strum, and each ___ represents a beat.

- Six Really Useful Strumming Patterns -

In this arrows notation, Strumming Pattern #2 looks like this:

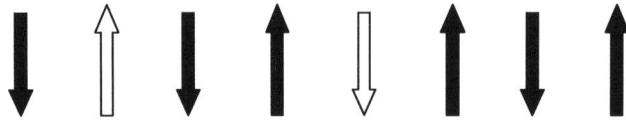

The white arrows represent 'miss-strums'; that is where you move your hand up or down without hitting the strings. Whilst playing a C chord (or any other chord you fancy playing), have a go at this strumming pattern whilst saying to yourself: "down, down-up, up-down-up" as you hit the strings. Play it over and over again, whilst making sure you keep a steady, slow beat. Your strumming hand should be moving steadily up and down just like it did before.

When the strumming pattern starts to feel comfortable, try speeding it up a little. With a little practice it'll start to become 'mechanical' (so that you can play it without having to think much about what your hand is doing).

When you're playing strumming patterns like this one, there is hardly any time between strums to move your fingers into different chord shapes. So what do you do? In this instance, you can simply play all of the strings open on the last up-strum of the pattern whilst you're moving you fingers into position for the next chord (as indicated by the O below). This may, perhaps, seem a little odd: "surely some of the notes in the open strings aren't in the right key for the song?" you may ask. Well, you'd be correct, but it doesn't seem to matter, as you only play them for a tiny amount of time. These open strums just seem to get swallowed up in the whole sound of the strummed ukulele.

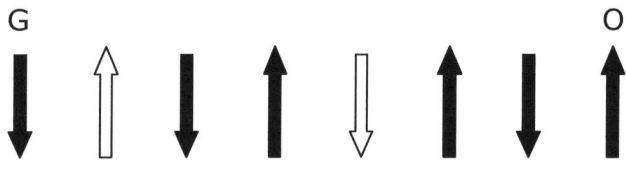

The Undertones' classic punk song 'Teenage Kicks' sounds great when played with this strumming pattern (see next page). I've arranged it in the key of C, so you know all of the chords in the song already, except Am ('A minor'). The chord diagram and a picture of the fingering for this chord are shown on the right. Minor chords sound sad or tense, and so,

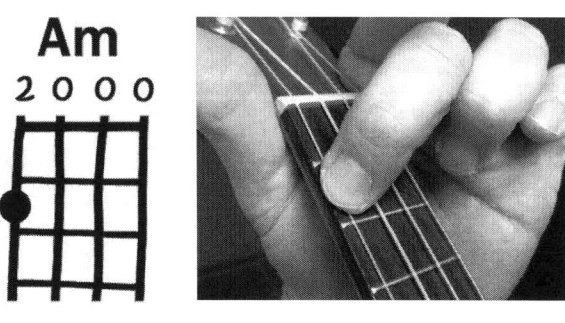

they can introduce a bit of extra atmosphere or emotion into a song. This is the minor chord that's often found in songs in the key of C, hence, it's said to be the 'related minor' for the key of C.

Incidentally, chords that are not minor chords (e.g., the C, F and G you've learned) are called 'major' chords. However, since this applies to the majority of chords played on the ukulele, the word 'major' is often not said.

- Six Really Useful Strumming Patterns -

Teenage Kicks (J. O'Neill)

Intro: C / / / / / / / Am / / / / / / / C / / / / / / / Am / / / / / / /

```
C
  A teenage dream's so hard to beat
Am
  Every time she walks down the street
C
  Another girl in the neighbourhood
Am
  Wish she we was mine, she looks so good
F
  I wanna hold her, wanna hold her tight
      G                              /  /
Get teenage kicks right through the night

C
  I'm gonna call her on the telephone
Am
  Have her over 'cause I'm all alone
C
  I need excitement, oh I need it bad
Am
  And it's the best I've ever had
F
  I wanna hold her wanna hold her tight
      G                              /  /
Get teenage kicks right through the night (alright!)
```

Solo: C / / / / / / / Am / / / / / / / C / / / / / / / Am / / / / / / /

(check out The Undertones' recording to get the full arrangement for this song)

- Six Really Useful Strumming Patterns -

Strumming Pattern #3

I use this strumming pattern a great deal. It sounds great in lots of different songs, but works particularly well with old American folk and country songs (e.g., Woody Guthrie, Leadbelly, The Carter Family, Hank Williams, and Jimmie Rodgers) and on skiffle songs. I sometimes refer to it as the 'skiffle pattern', as it was/is often used by skiffle players:

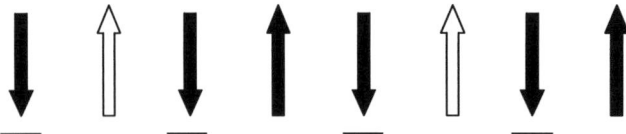

As you can perhaps see, this is actually a two-beat pattern that is played twice in each four-beat bar.

Nonsense words can be quite useful when describing strumming patterns. For example, this could be called a...

'jing, jing-a, jing, jing-a'

...strumming pattern (where each 'jing' represents a down-strum on a beat, and each '-a' represents an up-strum).

This pattern sounds great in songs with a bouncy, 'swing' or 'shuffle' rhythm. And if you wish to make these songs sound a bit 'beatier', you could try 'accenting' the second and third beat in each bar (called the 'backbeat') by hitting the strings a little harder than usual on these down-strums. Using the nonsense-word description, the pattern sounds like this:

'jing, **jing**-a, jing, **jing**-a'

...where the accented strums are shown in bold (say/play the bold 'jings' a bit louder).

This strumming pattern is reminiscent of the rhythm created by Johnny Cash and his band on many of their 1950s recordings. Have a go at playing it on this classic song of his: 'Folsom Prison Blues' (see next page).

- Six Really Useful Strumming Patterns -

Folsom Prison Blues (Johnny Cash)

Intro: D7 / / / / / / / G / / / / / /

```
   / G
```
I hear the train a comin'. It's rolling round the bend

And I ain't seen the sunshine since I don't know when
```
        C                                              G
```
I'm stuck in Folsom prison, and time keeps draggin' on
```
            D7                                G / / /  / / /
```
But that train keeps a-rollin' on down to San Antone

```
    / G
```
When I was just a baby my mama told me: "Son,

Always be a good boy, don't ever play with guns"
```
           C                         G
```
But I shot a man in Reno just to watch him die
```
           D7                                    G / / /  / / / /
```
When I hear that whistle blowing, I hang my head and cry

```
      Solo: G / / /  / / / /  / / / /  / / / /  / / / /  / / / /  / / / /  / / / /
            C / / /  / / / /  / / / /  / / / /  G / / /  / / / /  / / / /  / / / /
            D7 / / /  / / / /  / / / /  / / / /  G / / /  / / / /  / / / /  / / /
```

```
   / G
```
I bet there's rich folks eatin' from a fancy dining car

They're probably drinkin' coffee and smokin' big cigars
```
           C                               G
```
Well, I know I had it comin', I know I can't be free
```
           D7                                        G / / /  / / / /
```
But those people keep a-movin', and that's what tortures me

```
      Solo: G / / /  / / / /  / / / /  / / / /  / / / /  / / / /  / / / /  / / / /
            C / / /  / / / /  / / / /  / / / /  G / / /  / / / /  / / / /  / / / /
            D7 / / /  / / / /  / / / /  / / / /  G / / /  / / / /  / / / /  / / / /
```

```
   /   /   /   G
```
Well, if they freed me from this prison. If that railroad train was mine

I bet I'd move it on a little farther down the line
```
  C                                          G
```
Far from Folsom prison, that's where I want to stay
```
        D7                                       G / / /  / / / /
```
And I'd let that lonesome whistle blow my blues away

Outro: D7 / / / / / / / G / / / /

Strumming Pattern #4

I also use this strumming pattern a great deal, and it can be used as an alternative to Pattern #3 on much the same types of song.

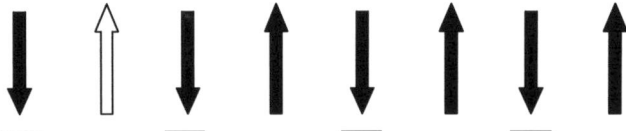

This could be called a...

'jing, jing-a, jing-a, jing-a'

...strumming pattern.

This pattern not only sounds great when used in songs with a bouncy, shuffle rhythm, but also songs with a straight, driving rhythm. When playing these rocky type songs it sounds really good if you accent the 'backbeat' as described with Pattern #3. Using the nonsense-word description, this pattern sounds like this:

'jing, **jing**-a, jing-a, **jing**-a'

On the next page you'll see a great Everly Brothers song that sounds just right with this strumming pattern, played with a bouncy, shuffle feel.

Unconvincing Everly Brothers ukulele tribute act!

- Six Really Useful Strumming Patterns -

Bye Bye Love (F. Bryant/B. Bryant)

Intro: G / / / / / / /

```
     C          G
  Bye bye love
     C          G
  Bye bye happiness
     C          G
  Hello loneliness
              D7      G
  I think I'm-a gonna cry-y
     C          G
  Bye bye love
     C          G
  Bye bye sweet caress
     C          G
  Hello emptiness
            D7       G
  I feel like I could di-ie
              D7       G  / / / G!
  Bye bye my love goodby-eye
```

```
            D7                      G
There goes my baby with-a someone new
            D7                 G
She sure looks happy, I sure am blue
              C               D7
She was my baby till he stepped in
                            G / / /  / / / /
Goodbye to romance that might have been
```

   CHORUS

```
              D7                        G
I'm-a through with romance, I'm a-through with love
                D7                  G
I'm through with a'countin' the stars above
              C               D7
And here's the reason that I'm so free
                          G / / /  / / / /
My lovin' baby is through with me
```

   CHORUS

Strumming Pattern #5
Here's another useful strumming pattern:

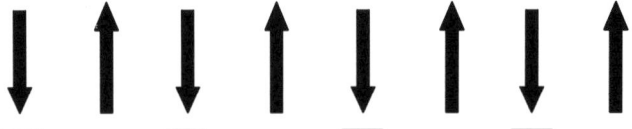

As you can see, with this pattern you're hitting the strings with every up and down movement of your strumming hand, and because of this, the pattern can sound a little uninteresting unless you accent the backbeat. When the backbeat is accented like this musicians sometimes describe this pattern as having a 'train rhythm', since it is reminiscent of the mechanical, driving sound of an old locomotive.

This could be called a...

'jing-a, **jing**-a, jing-a, **jing**-a'

...strumming pattern.

This pattern sounds really good when used in rocky songs with a straight, driving rhythm, but it also sounds great on many rockabilly/rock 'n' roll songs when given a bouncy, shuffle feel.

This strumming pattern works really well on Buddy Holly's song 'Maybe Baby', when played with a straight, driving rhythm (see next page). For this song you'll be using another 'minor chord': Em. The diagram for this chord can be seen on the right together with a photo of the standard fingering. This is the related minor in the key of G.

The chords in 'Maybe Baby' change pretty frequently compared with other songs we've looked at so far. This may be a little tricky to get the hang of at first. I'd suggest that you start off playing the song quite slowly, and only build up the speed of your strumming as the chord changes start to come smoothly.

- Six Really Useful Strumming Patterns -

Here's a little technical tip that can make playing this and similar chord progressions a little easier: If you compare a G with an Em you'll see that the only difference is the note that's played on the third string: with the G a note is played on the second fret, whilst with the Em a note is played on the fourth fret. You can take advantage of this similarity to make changing from the G to the Em a little easier and smoother. Whilst ordinarily you should find it easier to use the 'standard' fingering for an Em chord (shown on the previous page), if you're playing a G, you can change to Em simply by placing your little finger on the fourth fret of the third string. You can leave your first finger where it is on the third string – as it's now behind your little finger it isn't affecting the sound of the chord (see pictures on the right).

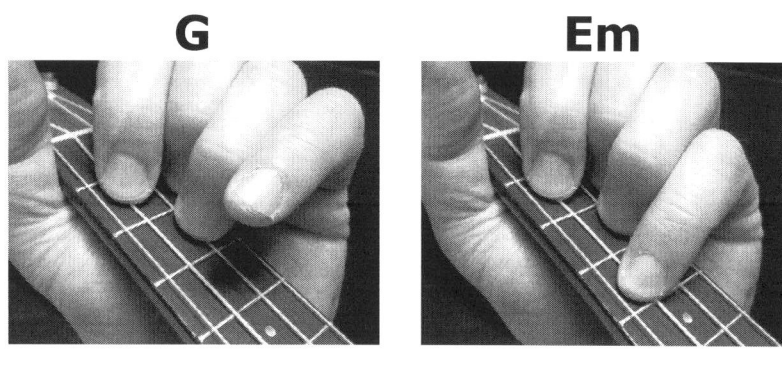

Maybe baby should put her jumper back on!

- Six Really Useful Strumming Patterns -

Maybe Baby (Hardin/Petty)

Intro: G / / / Em / / / G / / / Em / / / G / / / C / D7 / G / C / G D7 / /

```
G              Em
  Maybe baby, I'll have you
G              Em
  Maybe baby, you'll be true
G              C     D7  G   /  C/ G D7//
  Maybe baby, I'll have you for me—

G                 Em
  It's funny honey you don't care
G                    Em
  You never listen to my prayer
G              C    D7     G   /  C/ G//
  Maybe baby you will love me someday—
```

```
      /    C
   Well, you are the one that makes me glad
       G
   And you are the one that makes me sad
        C
   When someday you want me
            D7                    / /
   Well-a, I'll be there wait and see
```

Maybe baby, I'll have you
Maybe baby, you'll be true
Maybe baby, I'll have you for me—

   Solo: G / / / Em / / / G / / / Em / / / G / / / C / D7 / G / C / G / / /

   Well, you are the one that makes me glad
   And you are the one that makes me sad
   When someday you want me
   Well-a, I'll be there wait and see

Maybe baby, I'll have you
Maybe baby, you'll be true
Maybe baby, I'll have you for me—
```
G                C    D7 G   /   C/ G///
  Maybe baby, I'll have you for me—
```

- Six Really Useful Strumming Patterns -

Strumming Pattern #6
The sixth strumming pattern I'm going to show you is in 3/4 (waltz) timing, hence, it is a pattern that repeats every 3 beats. Start off by playing only down-strums on a G chord at a fairly fast pace, and count "**one**, two, three" (accent the one) over and over whilst you do this. Counting like this should help you to get the feel of this new time signature.

As you're playing only down-strums, and missing the strings as you move your hand up ready to play each down-strum, you're doing this:

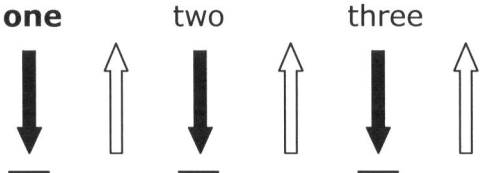

To play Strumming Pattern #3, all you have to do is replace the miss-strums after the 'two' and 'three' down-strums with up-strums, as follows:

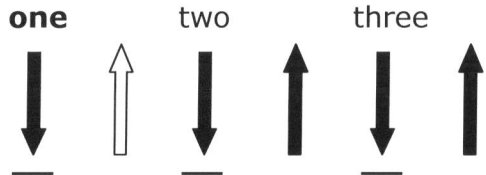

This could be called a...

'jing, jing-a, jing-a'

...strumming pattern.

This one sounds great when played on any song with a waltz timing, such as The Beatles' song, 'You've Got to Hide Your Love Away', from the film/album 'Help!' (see next page).

As you can see, the chords in this song change with almost every new bar, which may make it seem a little tricky. As with 'Maybe Baby', start off by playing it pretty slowly, and build up your speed gradually.

- Six Really Useful Strumming Patterns -

You've Got to Hide Your Love Away (Lennon/McCartney)

Intro: G / / / / /

```
 G    D7      F     G
Here I stand with head in hand
 C             F    C
Turn my face to the wall
 G    D7   F     G
If she's gone I can't go on
 C             F / /  C / /  D7 / /  / / /
Feeling two foot sma————————ll
 G    D7   F     G
Everywhere people stare
 C            F    C
Each and every day
 G    D7       F     G
I can see them laugh at me
 C             F / /  C / /  D7 / /  / / /  / / /  / / /
And I hear them s——————ay
```

```
       G            C             D7 / /  / / /  / / /  / / /
      Hey, you've got to hide your love aw————————ay
       G            C             D7 / /  / / /  / / /  / / /
      Hey, you've got to hide your love aw————————ay
```

```
 G       D7 F    G
How could I  even try
 C            F    C
I can never win
 G     D7    F     G
Hearing them, seeing them
 C             F / /  C / /  D7 / /  / / /
In the state I'm i————————n
 G     D7    F     G
How could she say to me
 C            F    C
Love will find a way
 G    D7   F      G
Gather round all you clowns
 C             F / /  C / /  D7 / /  / / /  / / /  / / /
Let me hear you s——————ay
```

```
       G            C             D7 / /  / / /  / / /  / / /
      Hey, you've got to hide your love aw————————ay
       G            C             D7 / /  / / /  / / /  / / / G
      Hey, you've got to hide your love aw————————ay
```

Six Really Useful Strumming Patterns

Changing Chords Part Way Through a Bar
When the chords in a progression change, they usually do it at the beginning of a bar. Since the strumming patterns I have described are one bar in length, this means that chord changes and strumming patterns tend to mesh together pretty well. However, occasionally, chords change part way through a bar (e.g., exactly half way). When this happens I tend to do one of two things:

1) I simply carry on with the strumming pattern, so that half is played with one chord and half with another chord. With Strumming Pattern #2, that looks like this:

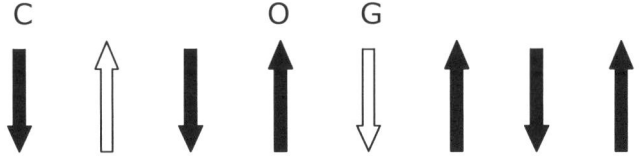

With this strumming pattern, you could play an open up-strum just before you get your fingers into position for the second chord in the bar (as indicated above by the O).

2) I play the first half of the strumming pattern twice, so that the first part is played with each chord, like this:

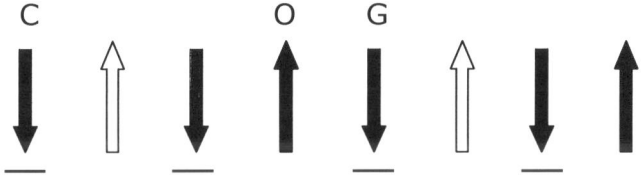

As with the first method, you could play an open up-strum just before you get your fingers into position for the second chord in the bar (as indicated).

Spot the odd one out!

12. Three Chord Tricks

As we've already seen, many songs (particularly folk, old country, blues and rock 'n' roll songs) can be played with just three chords, and for this reason, the chord progressions used with them are sometimes jokingly called 'three chord tricks'.

There are groups of three chords that go together well, and I will attempt to explain why. Knowing why certain chords are used together in songs can help you to learn and remember new songs more easily, and help you to work out the chords for a song for yourself (and not rely solely on chord sheets or songbooks).

As you've probably noticed, the chords C, F and G often go together in songs being played in the key of C. These three chords can be called the 1, 4 and 5 chords (sometimes written in roman numerals: *I, IV, V*). These numerical labels refer to the order in which the notes appear in the musical scale for the key in which a song is being played. Here are the notes in a C major scale, together with labels for the order of the notes:

1	*2*	*3*	*4*	*5*	*6*	*7*	*8*
C	D	E	F	G	A	B	C

Here you can see why the C, F and G are referred to as the 1, 4 and 5 chords in the key of C.

Similarly, for songs played in the key of G, the chords G, C and D often go together. In the key of G, these are, again, the 1, 4 and 5 chords:

1	*2*	*3*	*4*	*5*	*6*	*7*	*8*
G	A	B	C	D	E	F#	G

The most popular keys for ukulele songs tend to be C, G, D, A and F. This is because these songs can be played mostly or entirely with open chords (which tend to be easier, and often sound more fitting than moveable or 'bar' chords). Here are the groups of three chords that often go together in these five different keys:

Key	1	4	5
C	C	F	G7
G	G	C	D7
D	D	G	A7
A	A	D	E7
F	F	Bb	C7

The 5 chord is often played as a 'seventh' chord (although it doesn't have to be). Using a seventh chord can make the chord accompaniment to a song sound a little more interesting than using an ordinary, major chord – it adds a certain 'tension' to the musical accompaniment.

- Three Chord Tricks -

It's a good idea to learn which chords go together in these common keys. This way, for example, if someone says to you "Play along with me on this three chord trick song in the key of G", you will know that the song will contain the chords G, C and D (or D7).

It's not that important, but in case you wanted to know, in musical terminology the 1, 4 and 5 chords are known as the 'tonic', 'subdominant' and 'dominant' respectively. When the 5 chord is played as a seventh, it's called a 'dominant seventh'.

I find that it helps to understand and remember a chord progression if I liken it to a journey - the 1 is the 'home' chord, since it is usually where you start from, and it's usually where you return at the end of the chord progression. During the progression you may, for example travel to the 5 from the 1, travel to the 5 via the 4, or return to the 1 from the 5 directly or via the 4. To illustrate this notion, here is the chord progression used in the Lonnie Donegan, skiffle song, 'Putting On The Style', when played in the key of C:

```
    C                                          G7
    Sweet sixteen, goes to church just to see the boys
                                               C
    Laughs and screams and giggles at every little noise
                                               F
    Turns her face a little, then turns her head a while
        G7                                     C
    But everybody knows she's only putting on the style
```

This chord progression can also be written like this:

```
    I                                          V
    Sweet sixteen, goes to church just to see the boys
                                               I
    Laughs and screams and giggles at every little noise
                                               IV
    Turns her face a little, then turns her head a while
        V                                      I
    But everybody knows she's only putting on the style
```

This numerical notation shows the chord progression in a form that is independent from any key. As you can see, the progression begins on the 1 before climbing to the 5 and back home to the 1. Next, you climb up to the 5 again, via the 4, before finally returning home to the 1 again. The penultimate chord is the 5, and it's worth noting that this is very often the case in three chord tricks.

This 'journey' metaphor may seem weirdly poetic, but it helps me to remember chord progressions, and I've known many other musicians who think in a similar way. Maybe you do this already yourself?

- Three Chord Tricks -

Incidentally, this numerical way of presenting chord progressions is sometimes called the 'Nashville number system', since it is/was often used by arrangers and session musicians in recording studios in Nashville, Tennessee. It means that a musician can use a chord sheet in this notation to play a song in whatever key is appropriate to the band or singer, without having to re-arrange any written music.

It can be very useful to think in this 1-4-5 way, as it can enable you to transpose a song easily when necessary. For example, if you know a chord progression in the key of C, such as: C, F, C, G7, C, then if you know which chords are the 1, 4 and 5 in the keys of C and G, then you can easily transpose the progression to the key of G (which would make it: G, C, G, D7, G).

Quite a number of songs have what I think of as 'zigzag' chord progressions. This is where the chords switch back and forth as follows:

1 4 1 5 1 4 1 5 1

or sometimes...

1 5 1 4 1 5 1

This type of progression starts with, and is centred on, the 1, and switches back and forth between the 4 and the 1 and the 5 and the 1, and so on. Woody Guthrie's well-known song, 'This Land Is Your Land', is a good example of a folk song which uses a 'zigzag' chord progression. Here is the chorus of this song when played in the key of C:

```
   C              F                    C
 This land is your land and this land is my land
        G7                   C
 From California to the New York Island
              F                          C
 From the red wood forest to the Gulf Stream waters
      G7                      C
 This land was made for you and me
```

Notice how the 5 chord is played as a 'seventh'. The 'zigzag' idea refers simply to the order in which chords are played. Whilst this pattern is quite regular, the number of bars or beats for which you play a particular chord will usually vary between and within songs.

The traditional American folk song, 'Jesse James' also uses a zigzag chord progression. Over the page is a verse of this song arranged in the key of F. In this key we have Bb (see chord diagram and picture on right). As can be seen, with this chord you have to hold down the 1st and 2nd

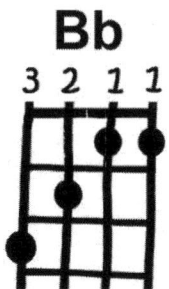 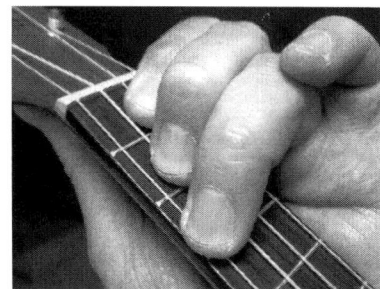

- Three Chord Tricks -

strings with the first finger. Some players find this chord shape a little tricky at first. If, for example, you struggle to make a clear note on the first string, or find yourself touching the second string with the second finger as it holds down a note on the third string, then you're not alone. As with any aspect of learning the ukulele, this should improve with practice, and perhaps after experimenting with different left hand thumb positions. As you can see in the photograph, I find it easier to make this chord shape if I move my thumb round to the back of the neck (instead of it sticking out like it usually is).

In the key of F we also have the C7, which is a very easy, one finger chord (see on right).

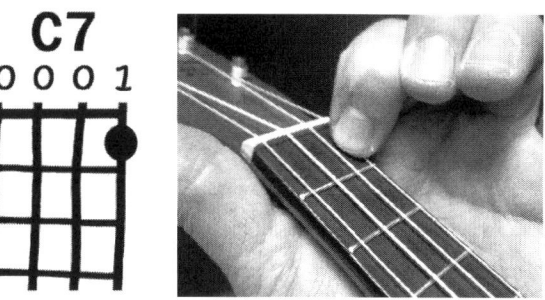

```
        F
Jesse James was a lad
      Bb         F
Who killed many a man
                    C7
He robbed the Glendale train
    F
He stole from the rich
        Bb        F
And he gave to the poor
           C7         F
He'd a hand and a heart and a brain
```

Johnny Cash's 'Folsom Prison Blues' (which we've already looked at in the key of C) is played using a chord progression that is reminiscent of the '12-bar blues' (strictly speaking it's a '24-bar blues' as each bar is doubled up...), which follows a zigzag pattern. Here's the first verse of this song when played in the key of F:

```
     F
I hear the train a comin'

It's rolling round the bend

And I ain't seen the sunshine since I don't know when,
    Bb                                           F
I'm stuck in Folsom prison, and time keeps draggin' on
    C7                                    F
But that train keeps a-rollin' on down to San Antone
```

Three chord songs that don't have a regular zigzag chord progression throughout, often feature a zigzag chord pattern at some point. For example, the traditional American folk song, 'Greenback Dollar'. The chorus of this song is presented on the right.

```
                        C
I don't want your greenback dollar
           F                C
I don't want your diamond ring
      F                C
All I want is your love darlin'
         G7             C
Won't you take me back again
```

- 55 -

- Three Chord Tricks -

The chords in this song are: 1 4 1 4 1 5 1. As you can see, after the first two chord changes, the progression follows a zigzag pattern.

Three chord tricks can be embellished a little by adding seventh chords in certain places within the progression. For example, here is the verse from 'Putting On The Style' that was presented earlier, with an added seventh chord:

```
      C                                          G7
   Sweet sixteen, goes to church just to see the boys
                                             C
   Laughs and screams and giggles at every little noise
                          C7              F
   Turns her face a little, then turns her head a while
        G7                                       C
   But everybody knows she's only putting on the style
```

Here, a C7 chord has been added in the third line, between the C and F chords. The inclusion of the 1 played as a seventh chord likes this, shortly before the chord changes from the 1 to the 4, creates a kind of musical tension, and in this way, seems to indicate to the listener that the chord is about to change. This tension is resolved when the chord eventually changes to the 4.

In the same way, you could add an F7 chord to the verses of 'Folsom Prison Blues' (see below). The F7 chord can be played in one of two different ways. As the chord diagram on the right shows, there is a three finger version (just the black dots), or a four finger version, where the fourth finger is added to the first string on the fourth fret (as indicated by the circle). With the four finger F7 each string produces a different note. Hence, it perhaps has a fuller sound than the three finger version, with which the same note is made on the first and fourth strings.

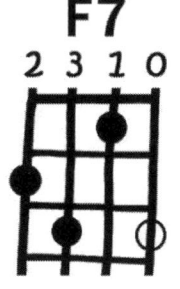 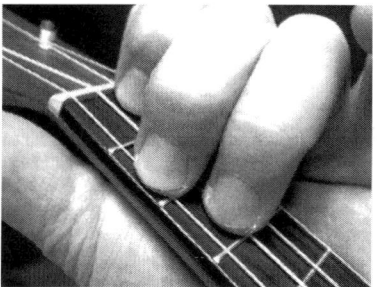

```
      F
   I hear the train a comin'

   It's rolling round the bend
                                      F7
   And I ain't seen the sunshine since    I don't know when,
        Bb                                            F
   I'm stuck in Folsom prison, and time keeps draggin' on
            C7                                    F
   But that train keeps a-rollin' on down to San Antone
```

Whilst we're looking at *three* chord tricks, it's worth noting that some songs manage to get by with only *two* chords. In these instances, the two chords are most often the 1 and the 5. Hank Williams' old country song, 'Jambalaya' is a good example of this. The first verse of Jambalaya when played in the key of D is shown on the next page.

- Three Chord Tricks -

The D and A7 chords that are used in this key can be seen in the chord diagrams and pictures below. There are two main ways of playing a D chord: one involves squeezing your first, second and third fingers all together onto the second fret (see chord diagram and picture on the left, below), and the other involves barring the strings on the second fret with the first finger and placing your fourth finger on the first string on the fifth fret (see chord diagram and picture on the right, below). As you can perhaps see, I have trouble making the non-barred D with my chunky fingers (on my soprano and concert ukes, anyway), and so, I tend to use the barred version. With the barred D each string produces a different note. Hence, it perhaps has a fuller sound than the non-barred version, with which the same note is made on the first and fourth strings. Notice how I place my thumb at the back of the neck when playing the barred D chord.

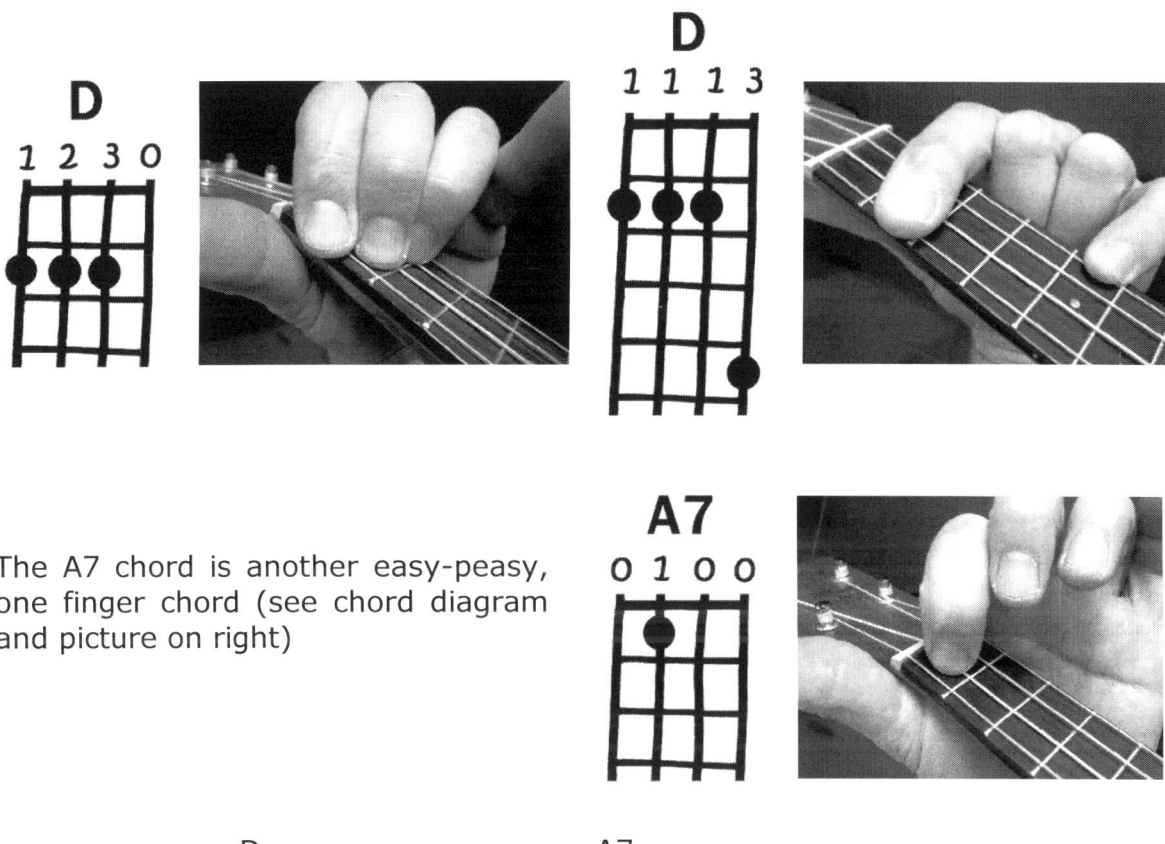

The A7 chord is another easy-peasy, one finger chord (see chord diagram and picture on right)

```
      D                        A7
Goodbye Joe, me gotta go, me oh my-oh
                                       D
Me gotta go pole the pirogue down the bayou
                                  A7
My Yvonne, the sweetest one, me oh my-oh
                              D
Son of a gun, well have big fun on the bayou
```

This isn't a simplified version of the song, it's simply how it's played. The old American folk song, 'Tom Dooley' is another example of a two chord (1 & 5) song. The chorus of Tom Dooley when played in the key of A is shown on the next page.

- Three Chord Tricks -

The A and E7 chords that are used in this key can be seen in the chord diagrams and pictures below. There's nothing too challenging about the A chord, but take care to avoid touching the open second string with your second finger when playing the E7.

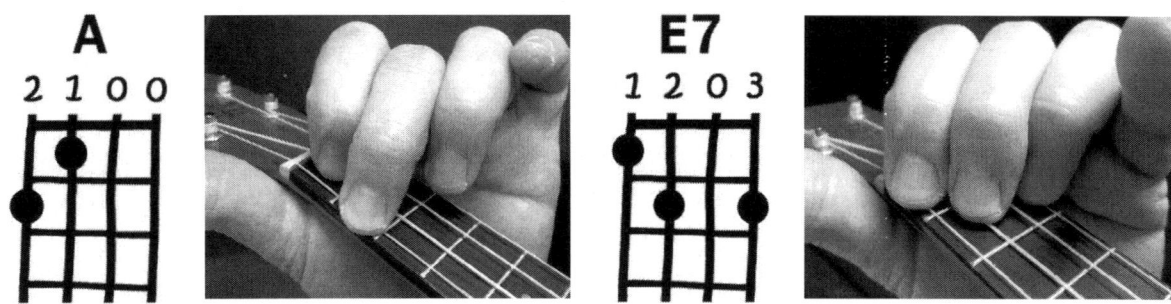

     A
Hang down your head, Tom Dooley
                         E7
Hang down your head and cry

Hang down your head, Tom Dooley
                     A
Poor boy, you're gonna die

The fact that these and many other songs get by with only the 1 and 5 chords illustrates how these are the most 'important' two chords in a three chord trick. The 4 chord often seems to act simply as a 'transition' chord. For example, it acts as the 'step up' from the 1 to the 5, or the 'step down' from the 5 to the 1. The 4 also seems to be used to add interest to a chord progression by breaking up a longish period where the 1 or the 5 chord are being played.

The version of the 12-bar blues chord progression used in Chuck Berry's 'Roll Over Beethoven' (and in many other blues and rock 'n' roll songs) illustrates both of these uses of the 4 chord. In this example, I've shown how the first verse of 'Roll Over Beethoven' would be played in the key of A (where D is the 4 or subdominant chord):

                A
Well I'm gon' write a little letter
         D   A   A7
I'm gonna mail it to my local DJ
     D
It's a jumpin' little record
               A
I want my jockey to play
    E7   D   A
Roll Over Beethoven, I gotta hear it again today

In the first version of the 12-bar blues chord progression I presented ('Folsom Prison Blues'), the first two lines of the song (the first 4 bars, that is) were played using the 1 chord only. In 'Roll Over Beethoven', however, these four

- Three Chord Tricks -

bars are broken up with the insertion of the 4 chord in the second line (the second bar). Also, in 'Roll Over Beethoven' I have added a 4 chord between the 5 and the 1 in the final line of the verse (acting as a 'step down').

With practice, it is possible to train your ear so that you can hear a song on a recording, and recognise when a 1, 4 or a 5 chord is being played. The more songs you learn, and the more you think about which chord is which in chord progressions you're playing, the more you'll be able to do this. In time, you should be able to jam along with a recording or with somebody who is playing a song you've never played before; you'll be able to anticipate when the chord is about to change, as well as which chord you're changing to (most of the time, at least).

The songs of Woody Guthrie, Leadbelly, the original Carter Family, Jimmie Rodgers and most Johnny Cash, are really good examples of the use of the three chord trick in folk, blues and country music. These artists rarely, if ever, used any more than three chords in their songs.

Prolific songwriter Harlan Howard once said:
"All you need to write a country song is three chords and the truth."

Lou Reed said:
"One chord is fine. Two chords is pushing it. Three chords and you're into jazz."

Extreme uke playing!

13. Alternative Tunings

As mentioned earlier, the re-entrant 'C tuning' is the standard ukulele tuning, and so, all of the musical ideas described in this guide assume that your uke is tuned this way. Some players, however, like to tune their ukuleles differently.

The D Tuning

The most popular alternative ukulele tuning is the 'D tuning': A D F# B. There are two versions of this:

1. **English tuning** – where each string is simply tuned one tone higher than with standard, C tuning;

2. **Canadian tuning** – this is the same as English tuning, except the A string (fourth string) is tuned an octave lower, making it lower in pitch than the D string. The Canadian tuning is sometimes used with concert and tenor ukes, but rarely with soprano ukes.

As each string makes a different note in comparison to standard tuning, every chord you play has a different name: a G becomes an A; a C becomes a D; an F becomes a G, and so on (each chord is a tone higher in pitch than in standard tuning).

People may choose to use a D tuning because they like the different sound it gives their ukulele (the higher pitch can make your uke sound a little brighter), or because they find that many songs they want to play are pitched wrongly for their singing voice. For example, a singer may struggle to reach the low notes in a song that's normally played in the key of C. As we've seen, C is a great key for the ukulele, because the chords typically used in this key are nice and easy to play. If the player tunes their ukulele to a D tuning, then they can still use these chord shapes, but they may now be able to sing those low notes without difficulty.

"Couldn't the player simply transpose songs into keys that suit their voice better?" you may ask. Well, the answer to that would be "yes". However, the chords in those other keys may not sound quite the same, or may be that little bit trickier to play. For example, a song arranged in the key of C may have the following chord progression:

C / / / Am / / / F / / / G7 / / /

When transposed into the key of D, these chords would be:

D / / / Bm / / / G / / / A7 / / /

Whilst D isn't the most difficult chord in the world to play, it *is* a little trickier than C (a one finger chord). Bm on the other hand (a two finger chord involving a three or four string bar ...which you'll see in the next chapter) is quite a bit trickier to play than Am (another one finger chord). Chords like C and Am, that include lots of open notes, also sound a little different to chords that include mostly or entirely fretted notes, like D and Bm.

- Alternative Tunings -

So, using a D tuning can make sense for some people some of the time. If you choose to use a D tuning, you'll be fine playing by yourself. However, you'll run into difficulty if you wish to jam with other ukulele players who are using standard tuning.

Personally, I use C tuning about 99% of the time. I do, however, have an old soprano ukulele that I leave in D tuning (English) in case of emergency. George Formby used ukuleles with different tunings like this: so that he could sing in different keys, but play pretty much everything with the same chord shapes.

You can tune your uke to English D tuning in just the same way as described earlier in the guide – you simply begin by tuning the third string to a D. Alternatively, you could use an electronic tuner.

Open Tunings
Some players tune their ukuleles so that a major chord is played when all four open strings are strummed. For example, if you tune your ukulele to G E C G, then the open strings make a C chord. If you put a finger across all of the strings on the first fret, you're now playing a C#. If you now move your finger to the second fret, you're playing a D; slide it up to the third fret, and you're playing an Eb, and so on. Of course, the chord shapes that you've learned so far will sound pretty odd if you play them using this tuning – you'll have to learn a whole new set of chord shapes if you wish to use this tuning for much.

Baritone Ukulele Tuning
Baritone ukuleles (the largest in the uke family) are tuned to D G B E. This is the same as the top four strings of a guitar, except the fourth string on a guitar is tuned to a lower D (lower in pitch than the third string). This tuning gives the baritone uke a guitar-like sound. You can use the same chord shapes with baritone tuning as you do with C tuning, although the chords have different names: a G is a D; a C is a G, an F is a D, etc. If you play guitar, then you'll already know these chords

Ancient Britons always took ukuleles into battle!

14. Moveable Chords

'Moveable chords' are chord shapes that can be played in different positions on the neck of the ukulele. Without realising it perhaps, you've already come across a few of these. Most ukulele players only use these to play chords that cannot be played using open chords shapes. Occasionally, however, they're used because they sound a little different to open chords (they're generally made up of higher pitched notes) or to create rhythmic effects (see next chapter on 'Percussive Strumming'). Even then, players will tend to avoid playing chords high up the neck (e.g., beyond the fifth fret), because the higher up the neck you go, the narrower the frets become (and the more difficult it can be to squeeze your fingers into place!). Also, if you're new to moveable chords it can be easy to lose your way high up the neck (and mess up a song by accidentally playing a chord shape on the wrong fret).

Moveable Bb Chord Shapes

The Bb chord we encountered earlier is played with a moveable chord shape. If you play this shape with your first finger on the first fret, then you're playing a Bb chord. However, if you play the same chord shape one fret up from its usual position (so that your first finger is now on the second fret), you're now playing a B chord; if you move it up one more fret, you're playing a C; one more fret up and you're playing a C# (or Db), and so on. Hence, with this one chord shape you can play lots of different chords (see picture above of a C# chord made with this shape).

It's possible to move this chord shape (and the other shapes explored in this chapter) up and down the neck like this because no open notes are being played. This means that the intervals (i.e., the differences in pitch) between the notes in the chord remain the same wherever you play the chord shape. If the chord shape included open notes (e.g., like an open G chord), then the intervals between the open note and the fretted notes in the chord would vary, according to where the chord shape is played on the neck.

With a few modifications to this moveable Bb shape you can create moveable Bb7 and Bbm shapes (see diagrams and pictures on next page). To play a Bb7 you bar all four strings with your first finger on the first fret and place your second finger on the second fret of the third string. To play a Bbm you bar the first, second and third strings with your first finger on the first fret (some players bar all four strings, as with the Bb7) and place your third finger on the third fret of the fourth string. These chord shapes can be used in the same way as the Bb shape.

- Moveable Chords -

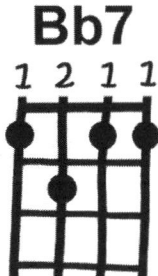 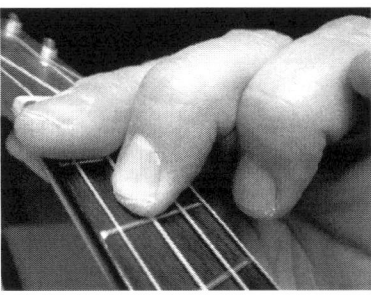 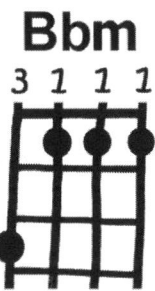 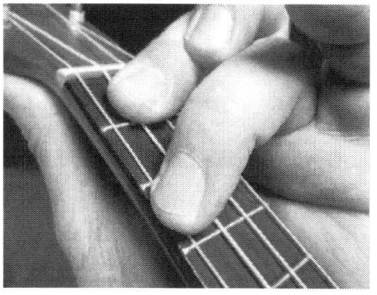

The table below shows the chords you can play with these three Bb shapes between the first and the seventh frets. Of course, whether the chord is a major, minor or seventh will depend upon the chord shape being played.

First finger position:	1st Fret	2nd Fret	3rd Fret	4th Fret	5th Fret	6th Fret	7th Fret
Chord being played:	A#/Bb	B	C	C#/Db	D	D#/Eb	E

Moveable D Chord Shapes

The barred D (which you've already seen) is also played with a moveable chord shape: if you play this chord shape one fret up from its usual position, you're now playing a D# (or Eb) chord; if you move it up one more fret, you're playing an E; one more fret up and you're playing an F, and so on. This chord can also be moved down one fret (so that the first finger is on the first fret) to make a C#/Db chord. Hence, as with the Bb shapes, with this chord shape you can play lots of different chords (see picture above of an E chord made with this shape).

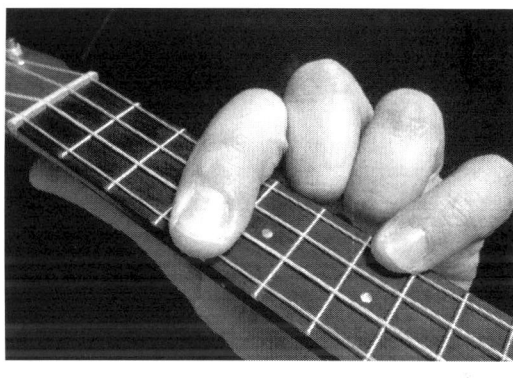

The barred D7 shape that we looked at a while back is also a moveable chord. If you slide it up one fret from its usual position, you're playing a D#7 (or Eb7) chord, and so on (see picture on right of an E7 chord made with this shape).

The table below shows the chords you can play with these D shapes between the first and the seventh frets.

First finger position:	1st Fret	2nd Fret	3rd Fret	4th Fret	5th Fret	6th Fret	7th Fret
Chord being played:	C#/Db	D	D#/Eb	E	F	F#/Gb	G

- Moveable Chords -

Moveable E Chord Shapes

Another moveable chord that you may find useful is shown on the left. Let's call this a moveable E shape. As can be seen, when your first finger is on the second fret, you're playing an E; when it's on the third fret, you're playing an F; when it's moved down to the first fret, you're playing an Eb (see picture on right of an F chord).

This moveable E chord can be tricky to play though. Perhaps you can see how my fingers are struggling to make the chord shape in the photograph? For this reason, I never use this shape; I use the moveable D shape instead (e.g., to play D# and E chords).

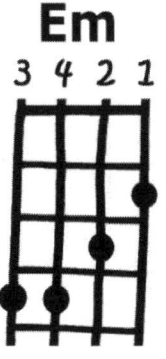 

With a slight modification to this moveable E shape you can create a moveable Em shape (see diagram and picture on the right).

If you have chunky fingers like me though, you may find this shape quite tricky. Because of this, when playing an Em I use the open chord shape presented earlier in the guide.

Some uke players who struggle with moveable shapes like these (that involve squeezing four fingers into a small space on the fingerboard) get around the problem by playing three finger versions of the chord shape. A moveable, three finger version of the Em shape can be played using the first, second and third fingers on the first, second and third strings (as with the open version of the chord). As indicated by the X in the chord diagram on the right, the fourth string is not played. This string is 'dampened' using the thumb, as shown in the photograph of an Ebm chord (on the left).

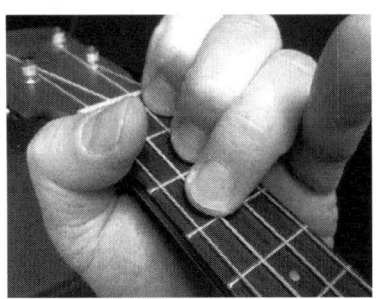

To dampen a string you simply touch it to prevent it from ringing out. A dampened string will make a dull, 'plunk' sort of noise when strummed as part of a chord, but this will be barely audible over the sound of the three fretted notes. Of course, having fewer fretted notes means that this chord shape won't sound as 'full' as the four finger version ...but sometimes we just have to make do.

- Moveable Chords -

The table below shows the chords that can be played using these E shapes between the first and the seventh frets.

First finger position:	1st Fret	2nd Fret	3rd Fret	4th Fret	5th Fret	6th Fret	7th Fret
Chord being played:	Eb	E	F	F#/Gb	G	G#/Ab	A

Moveable G Chord Shape

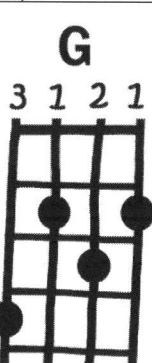

The G chord shape used up to this point in the guide is an open chord. As it contains on open fourth string it doesn't sound right when moved up the neck. There is, however, a way of playing a G with a moveable chord shape (see diagram on the right). To play this chord shape you bar the first, second and third strings with your first finger on the second fret and place your second and third fingers on the second and fourth strings as indicated.

If you play the same chord shape one fret up from the position shown in the diagram (so that your first finger is now on the third fret), you're now playing a G#/Ab chord; if you move it up one more fret, you're playing an A; one more fret up and you're playing an A# (or Bb), and so on. This chord can also be moved down one fret (so that the first finger is on the first fret) to make an F#/Gb chords.

The picture above shows an A chord being played with this chord shape, and the table below shows the chords that can be played using this shape between the first and the seventh frets.

First finger position:	1st Fret	2nd Fret	3rd Fret	4th Fret	5th Fret	6th Fret	7th Fret
Chord being played:	F#/Gb	G	G#/Ab	A	A#/Bb	B	C

Using Moveable Chords

Three chord tricks arranged in the key of G, like the chord progression in 'Bye Bye Love', can be played fairly easily with entirely moveable chords. Have a go at playing the chords from the verses of this song (see below): play the D7 using a barred D7 shape; play the G using the barred G shape; and play the C using the Bb shape (with your first finger on the third fret).

```
Verse:  D7 / / /  / / / /  G / / /  / / / /
        D7 / / /  / / / /  G / / /  / / / /
        C / / /   / / / /  D7 / / / / / / /
        / / / /   / / / /  G / / /  G!
```

- 65 -

How does it sound? Does it sound different to the version you've played using open chords? This is a good chord progression for practicing these moveable chord shapes and changing between them. Keep at it until it starts to sound nice and clean.

If I now asked you to play 'Bye Bye Love' in F#, then you might think I was asking too much. However, if you've managed to play this song in G, then you can easily play it in F# ...or Ab for that matter. All you have to do is shift the whole chord progression down or up one fret. If you play each chord one fret lower than you did in the key of G, then you would be playing the song in F# (you'd be playing: F#, B & C#7); if you play each chord one fret higher, then you would be playing the song in Ab (you'd be playing: Ab, C# & Eb7). Here we see one of the benefits of using moveable chords: easy transposition. If you're feeling brave, why not have a go at transposing another three chord song that you've played in the key of G (e.g., 'Folsom Prison Blues' or 'Maybe Baby')?

Some Final Thoughts

When you've become familiar with the moveable chords presented in this chapter, you'll not only know how to play lots of different chords (36 of them!), you'll also know different ways of playing the same chords. For example, you'll know three different ways of playing a C chord (an open C; a C using the Bb moveable chord shape; and a C using the barred G chord shape).

These different ways of playing a chord are called 'chord inversions' – we've looked at three inversions of a C chord. Usually, it makes sense to play the easiest inversion of a chord, which is usually an open chord. For example, it would be quite awkward to play a Dm using the Bbm moveable chord shape (with your first finger up on the fifth fret) in the middle of a chord progression that contains open chords and moveable chords played on lower frets. Instead, you would probably play Dm as shown in the chord diagram and picture on the right. Incidentally, Dm is the 'related minor' in the key of F.

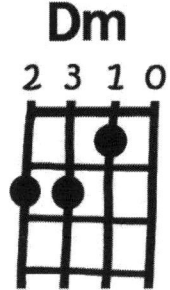 

So far, we've looked at some of the most used open chords, and the most useful moveable chords. There are lots more moveable and open chords though. It wouldn't make sense to consider them all here in detail. However, comprehensive tables of chords are presented at the back of this guide. If you're learning a new song (e.g., from a chord sheet or songbook), and you don't know a chord featured in the song, you should be able to find it in these tables.

15. Percussive Strumming

Earlier in the guide we looked at different ways of making rhythms on the ukulele by strumming up and down, playing miss-strums, and by accenting strums (see 'Six Really Useful Strumming Patterns'). Another way to create different rhythmic effects is to use 'percussive strums'. I use three different methods to create these, depending on the types of chords I'm playing or the sound I'm trying to make. Two of these methods involve strumming the ukulele with the right hand, but 'dampening' the strings with the left. To dampen strings with the left hand you simply touch them instead of pressing them all the way down to the fretboard or letting them ring out as open notes. As mentioned previously, if you do this, the strings make a kind of deadened 'plunk' sound instead of a ringing note. The third percussive strumming method involves dampening the strings with the right hand.

Percussive Method #1
If you're playing moveable chords, such as the Bb, barred D or barred G shapes, then playing percussive strums can be fairly straight-forward. Whilst strumming these chords you simply relax the fingers on your left hand so they remain touching the strings in the shape of the chord, but are no longer holding them down onto the fretboard.

Here's a handy strumming pattern for you to have a go at using this method:

Strumming Pattern #7
Pick your favourite moveable chord and strum up and down with a straight rhythm at a moderate speed, as shown here:

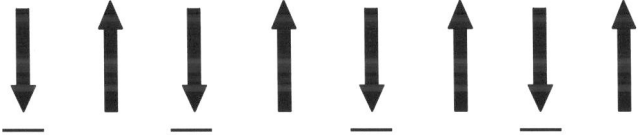

...then, try relaxing your left hand a little on the down-strums that fall on beats two and four as shown below (in grey).

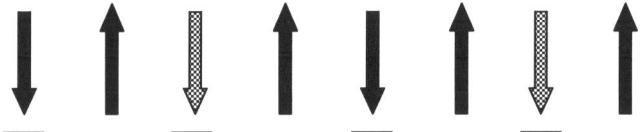

The percussive strums fall on the 'back beat', and so this pattern sounds great in beaty, rock and pop tunes irrespective of tempo (try playing it slow and steady, then try it fast and frantic). This is actually the same pattern as Strumming Pattern #5, except the backbeat is emphasised by percussive strums instead of accented (louder) strums. This pattern sounds like:

'jing-a, chick-a, jing-a, chick-a'

...and it can be played with a straight or a shuffle rhythm.

- Percussive Strumming -

You may find that you don't manage to dampen all of the strings at the same time on these ('chick') down-strums, so that one or two strings are still ringing out. If this happens, slow your strumming right down and look closely at your left hand whilst you're playing, to see if you can determine which finger is to blame. With practice you should be able to iron out this problem.

This percussive strumming method can also be employed with open chords, such as the F, E7 and Dm (see chord diagrams on the right). These chords all have single open strings that occur to the right of a fretted string (when looking at a chord diagram). This means that when you relax your fingers you can not only dampen the fretted strings, but also dampen the open strings. Depending upon the position of your left hand on the neck of the uke (e.g., thumb at the back vs. thumb sticking out) or the size of your fingers, this might occur quite naturally. Have a go at playing Strumming Pattern #7 with each of these chords. Are you able to dampen all of the strings? If not, try it again, but this time twist your hand ever so slightly towards the first string (i.e., to the right when looking at a chord diagram) as you relax your fingers, and in this way, allow your fingers to touch the open strings and dampen them.

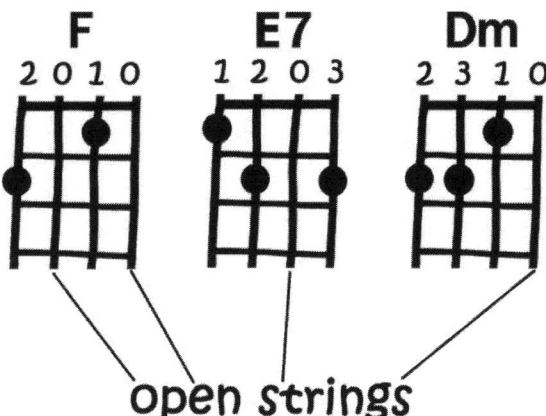

If you've got to grips with percussive strumming using open chords like these, then you may also be able to apply this method with open chords that include two or three adjacent open strings (provided they are to the 'right' of fretted strings); for example, A and Am. With these chords you may need to twist your hand around a little more in order to dampen the strings that are furthest away from your finger(s).

Now try out this percussive strumming method and Strumming Pattern #7 in a song. A song played entirely with moveable chords and/or the type of open chords discussed above would be best for now. How about a twelve-bar blues chord progression in the key of G? ...'Bye Bye Love', 'Folsom Prison Blues' and 'Maybe Baby' would fit the bill too!

Percussive Method #2
When you're playing open chords such as C, G and Em (i.e., those with open strings to the 'left' of any fretted strings), relaxing your fingers on the fretboard will leave open strings to ring out, and will prevent you from playing a completely percussive strum. For this reason, I often use an alternative percussive strumming method. You may also prefer to use this alternative method if you find dampening strings with open chords such as F, E7 and Dm a little tricky as well.

- Percussive Strumming -

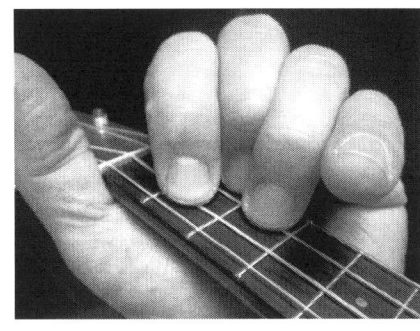

Most chords are played on the ukulele using the first, second and third fingers. This leaves the fourth finger free to help you to make percussive effects. For example, to play an open G you use your first, second and third fingers to make the chord shape shown in the picture on the left. Notice how my little finger is just hanging around with nothing to do. Well, if you bring your little finger

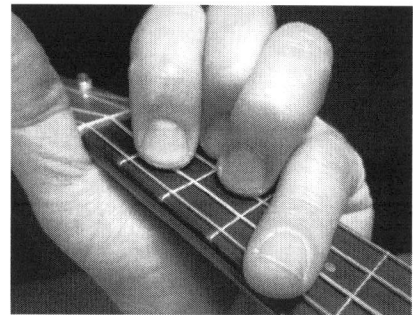

down towards the fretboard so that it dampens all four strings, you can use it to create percussive strums (see picture on right). To do this, you leave your fretting fingers exactly as they are (don't relax or move them at all). Remember just to touch the strings with your little finger to stop them ringing (don't press them down onto the fretboard).

This can be done fairly easily with most open chords. To the right are pictures showing what this looks like with C and A chord shapes.

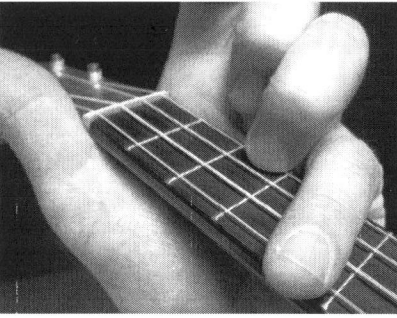
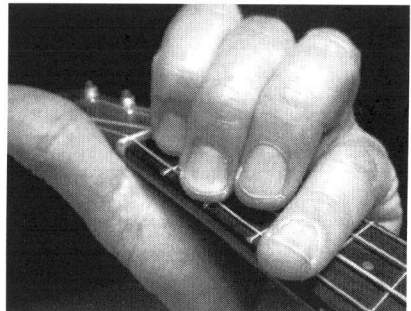

Now have a go at playing strumming pattern #7 using this percussive method. Then, try out the strumming patterns presented below (#8, #9 and #10) first with Percussive Strum Method #1, then with Method #2.

Strumming Pattern #8
This one-bar pattern has more percussive strums than actual strums! It can be used in reggae songs, or used to give a song a reggae feel. It can be played with a straight rhythm or with a bouncy, shuffle feel (to suit the tune):

Try playing this pattern on a folk song like Bob Dylan's 'Blowin' in The Wind' (presented earlier) to see how easy it is to give a song an interesting new feel.

- Percussive Strumming -

Strumming Pattern #9
Here's another reggae-style strumming pattern. This song has only two actual strums!

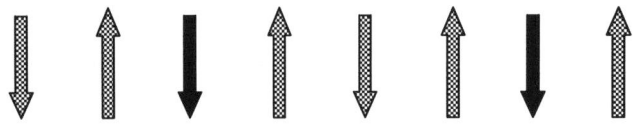

As can be seen, it's the same as pattern #8, but the up-strum after beat two is now a percussive strum. This can also be played with a straight rhythm or with a bouncy, shuffle feel (to suit the song).

Strumming Pattern #10
Down-strums, miss-strums and percussive strums can be combined to create some really impressive, rhythmic effects. This one-bar strumming pattern is the same as pattern #2, but with three percussive strums added:

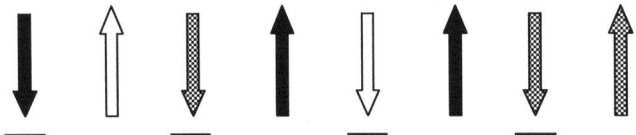

To get to grips with this rhythm, start off by playing the "down, down-up, up-down-up" of Strumming Pattern #2 quite slowly. As you did before, say these words to yourself as you're playing the rhythm. Then, add the percussive strums on the words that have been underlined: "down, <u>down</u>-up, up-<u>down</u>-up". As with Pattern #7, the percussive strums fall on the 'back beat', and so this sounds great in beaty, rock and pop tunes. Elvis Presley's 'Hound Dog' sounds really good when played with this strumming pattern.

Percussive Method #3
With this strumming method you dampen the strings to make a percussive effect by gently touching them with the soft, fleshy edge of your right hand whilst strumming with your index finger (see pictures on right). You continue to play chords as normal with your left hand. This method works really well with strumming patterns like #7 and #10 (but less well with patterns #8 and #9, which have more percussive strums than normal strums).

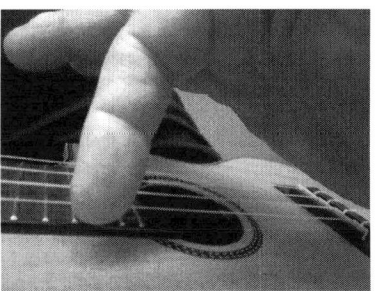

Usual position of my hand when strumming with index finger.

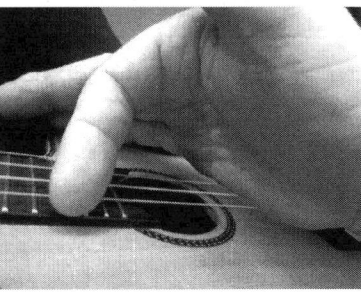

Placing the edge of my hand on the strings between the bridge and sound hole, and strumming downwards with index finger.

16. Rhythm Soloing

Some songs can be spiced up a little with the inclusion of an instrumental break or 'solo' ...usually somewhere around the middle. On the ukulele there are two main options: (1) solos that include single- or double-note expressive, melodic phrases; or (2) solos that involve playing chords in an interesting, rhythmic manner. If you wish to play the first type of solo, then you'll usually need at least one other instrument to accompany you during the solo. Without such accompaniment the music you're playing can seem a bit empty or appear to change pace in comparison to strummed accompaniment of lyrics before and after the solo.

If you wish to play the second type of solo, then you don't need this accompaniment: you can fill in any gaps with chords and rhythms, and in this way keep the momentum of the song rolling along. These solos sound good when accompanied by other players too though. For these reasons, and as this is a 'strummer's guide', in this chapter I'll give direction in playing these rhythm solos. I'll also give a few tips on how to embellish other parts of a song using short rhythmic 'fills'.

If you want to see and hear fantastic rhythm solos on the ukulele, then you need look no further than George Formby. Whilst he played his solos in jazzy, music hall style songs, rhythm solos can be played to good effect in many different types of music. There are some excellent ukulele players around who specialise in playing in the exact style of George Formby, but I'm not one of those. However, I often play rhythm solos that are inspired by his technique in punk, country, rock 'n' roll and skiffle tunes, etc. You may think that rhythm solos don't belong in this type of music: well, have a listen to the rhythmic guitar solos of, for example, Buddy Holly, Johnny Ramone and Bo Diddley, and hopefully you'll hear what I mean.

First of all I'm going explain how to play two fancy strumming techniques that George Formby often used (the 'split strum' and the 'triple strum'), then I'll give you some pointers on how to put these together with what you know already in order to create your own, original and exciting rhythm solos. This can be great fun, and it's nowhere near as difficult as it may sound.

The Split Strum
The 'split strum' is one of a number of special strumming patterns that can be used to create rhythmic chord solos – it isn't the type of pattern that's played repeatedly when accompanying a song.

When you play the split strum you create a 'syncopated' rhythm – that is, a rhythm where stresses or accents are placed where they wouldn't normally occur. Syncopated rhythms are used in many different types of music (e.g., ragtime, jazz and different forms of dance music, old and new).

Before attempting the split strum you should ideally be familiar with some of the strumming patterns I've previously introduced, and also familiar with strumming the ukulele using your index finger – whilst it's possible to play the split strum with a pick, this is a little trickier and it can be difficult to achieve the desired sound.

The split strum is four beats long. Using the up and down arrow notation introduced previously, the split strum looks like this:

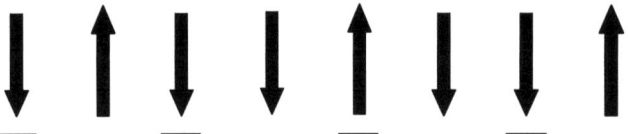

...and using a nonsense word description, the split strum sounds like this:

'jing-a, dee-**jing**-a, dee-**jing**-a'

As before, each 'jing' represents a down-strum, each '-a' represents an up-strum, and accented/stressed strums are shown in bold type. Unlike before, however, a 'jing' doesn't always fall on the beat and an '–a' doesn't always fall in between the beats. For this strum I have also introduced the 'dee', which is a down-strum that comes immediately before a jing.

For songs played on the ukulele in 4/4 time (i.e., those with four beats in each bar) there are usually two stressed strums which are played on beats two and four (i.e., the 'back beat'). With this strum, however (as can be seen from the bold jings), there are three stressed strums instead of two: these are on beats one and four, and in between beats two and three. Here we see the syncopated character of this strumming pattern. The split strum sounds great when it's played two or more times in succession.

This description probably makes the split strum sound more complicated and difficult to play than it actually is. As with learning any new strumming pattern, playing the split strum will come with just a little practice.

Start off by making a C chord with your left hand, and play the up- and down-strums in the strumming pattern three or four times in succession, quite slowly. If it helps, say the '**jing**-a, dee-**jing**-a, dee-**jing**-a' nonsense words to yourself as your strumming. Remember to strum a little harder on the jings (shown in bold) than on the other strums. All of the strums should be evenly spaced (two per beat). Repeat this exercise until the strumming pattern starts to feel mechanical and you can hear the syncopated rhythm you're creating. Then, speed up a little, and repeat the exercise ...and gradually continue speeding up until eventually you're playing the split strum as fast you can.

- Rhythm Soloing -

Now try playing the first five bars of the solo from Buddy Holly's 'Maybe Baby' (shown within the box) using the split strum:

Solo: G / / / Em / / / G / / / Em / / / G / / / C / D7 / G / C / G / / /

(play Strumming Pattern #5 in the last three bars)

In this way, you can start to turn a simple chord progression into an interesting rhythmic ukulele solo.

The Triple Strum

The 'triple strum' is another special strumming pattern that can be used to create rhythmic chord solos. It can also be used as a 'fill' or embellishment, for example, between the verses and choruses of a song. Like the 'split strum' it isn't the type of pattern that's played repeatedly when accompanying singing. The split strum and the triple strum sound great together – they're probably the two most common 'special' strumming patterns, and were often used to good effect by George Formby in solos.

Before attempting the triple strum you should ideally be familiar with some of the strumming patterns I've previously introduced, and also familiar with strumming the ukulele using your index finger – it isn't really possible to play the triple strum with a pick.

The triple strum, as the name suggests, involves playing three strums – these are played in the space of one beat, and fill the space where one or two strums would usually be played. It works particularly well in songs where you're using strumming patterns like #1, #3 or #4 (see 'Six Really Useful Strumming Patterns'). To use a nonsense word description, the triple sounds like: 'diddle-ee' (three syllables: did-dle-ee). The three syllables of the word correspond to the three strums in the pattern.

The first of the three strums (the 'did') is a down-strum, and is played with the index finger – this strum should fall on the beat (the 'down beat'). The second strum (the 'dle') is also a down-strum, and is played with the thumb. The third strum (the '-ee') is an up-strum, and is played with the index finger. Here's what the triple strum looks like in the arrows notation:

'did dle –ee'

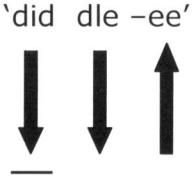

When playing the triple strum you should hold your right hand in the usual position for strumming with the index finger (see 'Strumming Techniques'). Previously, I've suggested that when strumming with the index finger you should keep your thumb out of the way by tucking it in or sticking it out at right angles to the index finger. If you tuck your thumb in, then just before playing the triple strum you'll need to stick your thumb out in order to get it ready to strum downwards. Make sure that you're strumming from the wrist (and not the elbow).

- Rhythm Soloing -

Make a C chord with your left hand and practice the three strums of the triple strum quite slowly (so that it's around 1 to 1½ seconds in duration). Try to make a smooth downward motion when playing the down-strums with the index finger and thumb, and also make the up-strum with the index finger follow on smoothly. The three strums should be equally spaced. If it helps, say 'diddle-ee' to yourself at the same time as you're playing the three strums. Repeat this exercise until the three strums and up and down movement of your hand start to feel smooth and mechanical.

Now try inserting the triple strum in between some down-strums using Strumming Pattern #1, like this:

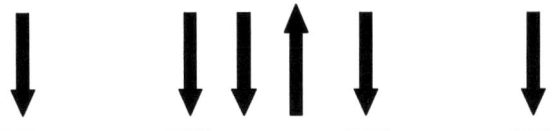

Here, the triple strum has been inserted on beat 2 of this 4-beat bar. This should sound like:

'jing, diddle-ee, jing, jing'

Play this one-bar strumming pattern over and over (8 or more times). Repeat this exercise until the whole one-bar pattern starts to feel fluent and mechanical.

The triple strum can be inserted on any beat of a bar. When played on the second beat (as above) it works really well as a fill. If a song has pauses in between verses or chorus (as many songs do) you could use the triple strum in the bar immediately preceding the start of a verse or chorus. For example, after each chorus in Lonnie Donegan's skiffle classic, 'Putting On the Style' there is a four bar pause – try inserting a bar containing a triple strum in the last of these bars (shown within the rectangle below):

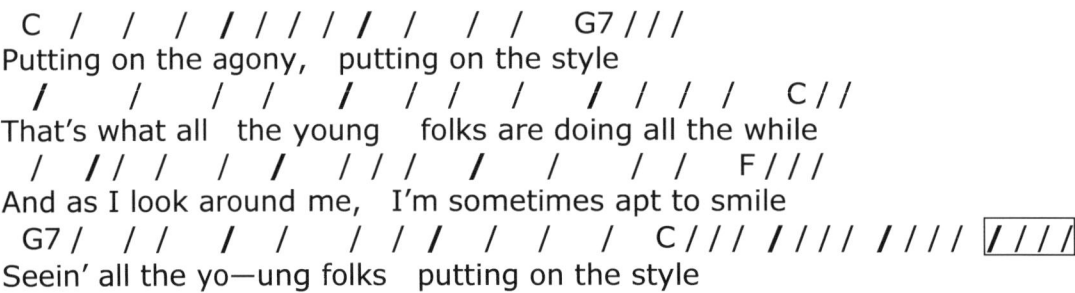

(the full lyrics and chords to this song are presented later)

- Rhythm Soloing -

You could also use the triple strum as a fill when there is a pause between the lines within a verse or chorus. For example, in the verses of 'Putting On the Style' you could insert fills in the bars between each line (again, shown within the rectangles below):

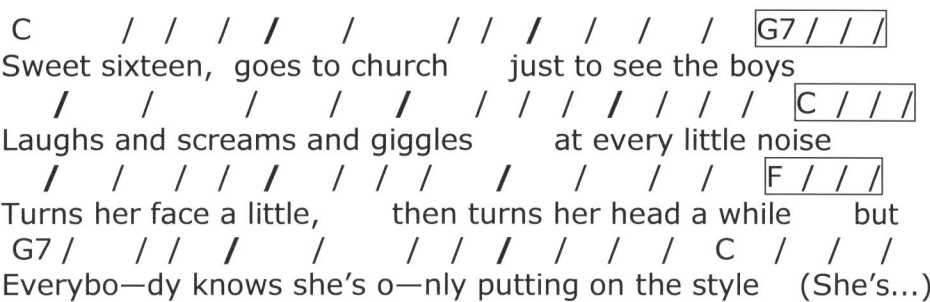

The triple strum also sounds great as a fill when played on beat 4. For example, if you're using Strumming Pattern #3 (aka the 'skiffle pattern'):

'jing, **jing**-a, jing, **jing**-a'

...you might insert it like this:

'jing, **jing**-a, jing, diddle-ee'

...so that the triple strum replaces the 'jing-a' on beat 4.

As before, play this one-bar strumming pattern over and over (8 or more times), and repeat this exercise until the whole one-bar pattern starts to feel fluent and mechanical. As suggested above, you could use the triple strum like this in the bar immediately preceding the start of a verse a chorus.

Now try playing the following two-bar pattern:

...which sounds like:

'jing, diddle-ee, jing, jing, diddle-ee, jing, jing, jing'

Here, the triple strum has been inserted on beat 2 of the first bar, and on beat 1 of the second bar. The stress associated with the second of these triple strums gives this two-bar pattern a syncopated feel. Once again, play this strumming pattern over and over until the pattern starts to feel fluent and mechanical. This pattern works very well as the basis for a rhythm solo.

Try playing a solo for 'Putting in the Style' using this two-bar, triple strum pattern. Here are the chords:

- Rhythm Soloing -

```
Solo:  C / / /  / / / /  / / / /  G7 / / /
       / / / /  / / / /  / / / /  C / / /
       / / / /  / / / /  / / / /  F / / /
       G7 / / /  / / / /  / / / /  C / / /
```

As with the split strum, in this way you can start to turn a simple chord progression into an interesting ukulele rhythm solo. When you're starting to feel comfortable with the triple strum, try experimenting by inserting it in different positions within the bars of this chord progression to create interesting and syncopated effects.

Cliff "Ukulele Ike" Edwards confuses uke with flute...

- Rhythm Soloing -

Putting On the Style (Lonnie Donegan)

Intro: C / / / / / / /

```
 C                                         G7
Sweet sixteen, goes to church just to see the boys
                                         C
Laughs and screams and giggles at every little noise
                                         F
Turns her face a little, then turns her head a while
     G7                                   C  /  /  /
But everybody knows she's only putting on the style   (She's...)

       C                             G7
    Putting on the agony, putting on the style
                                         C
    That's what all the young folks are doing all the while
                                         F
    And as I look around me, I'm sometimes apt to smile
       G7                             C / / / / / / / / / / / / /
    Seein' all the young folks putting on the style

  /    C                                    G7
Well, the young man in the hot-rod car, driving like he's mad
                                         C
With a pair of yellow gloves he's borrowed from his dad
                                         F
He makes it roar so lively just to see his girlfriend smile
 G7                                   C  /  /  /
But she knows he's oh-oh-only putting on the style  (Yeah...)
```

        CHORUS

```
 C                                    G7
Preacher in the pulpit roars with all his might
                                         C
Sings "Glory Hallelujah" puts the folks all in a fright
                                         F
Now, you might think it's Satan that's coming down the aisle
       G7                                       C  /  /  /
But it's only our poor preacher, boys, it's putting on his style  (Yeah...)
```

        CHORUS

Rhythm Soloing

Putting it All Together

A good rhythm solo should ideally have a structure (e.g., a beginning, a middle, and an ending). In this way, you can grab the attention of your audience and keep them listening till the end of the solo. For example, it can sound great to start the solo off very simply, such that for the first few bars you just play down-strums on the beat, or play one of the other straight-forward strumming patterns presented in this guide. After that you might play the split strum and intersperse it with some triple strums, creating exciting, expressive and syncopated effects, but still sticking to the basic chord progression of the song. Finally, you could end the solo with some syncopated triple strumming before the singing begins again.

At first, you may find it helpful to plan a solo you want play, bar by bar, something like I've done below. This is the chord progression from Woody Guthrie's 'This Land Is Your Land':

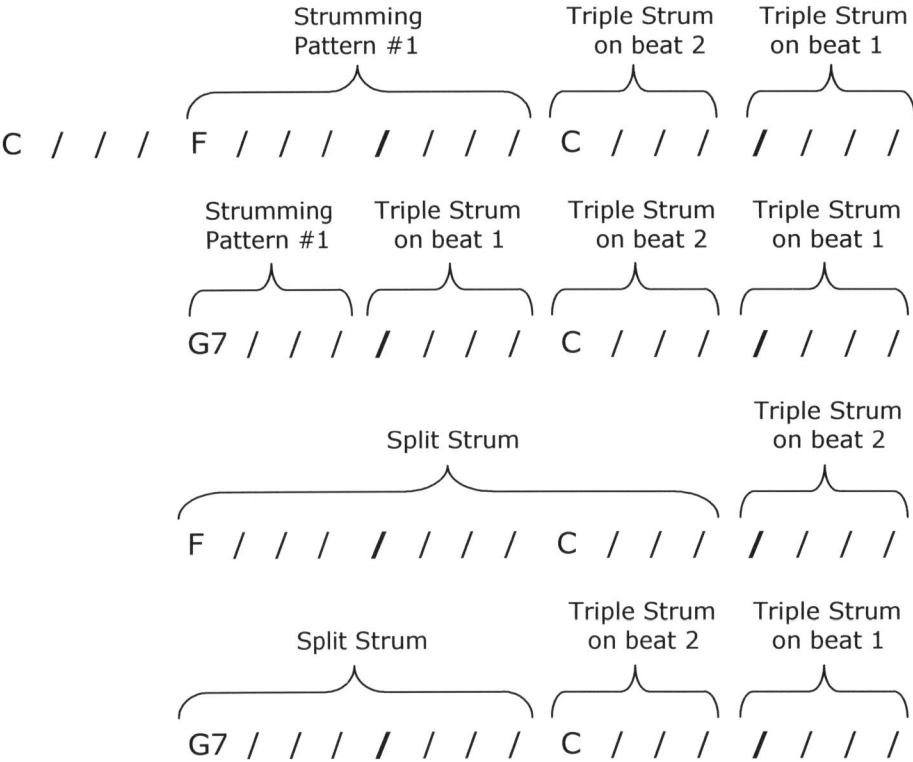

In the end, creating and playing a good rhythm solo is down to your own skill and creativity.

17. A Closer Look at Chords

This chapter is for those who'd like to know something about how and why different combinations of notes are put together to make different types of chord. Knowing a little about this will deepen your understanding of how the music you play is constructed, ...and this can help you to learn new songs more easily. As you'll see, there's a pretty simple logic to it all.

Major Chords
A basic major chord is made up of three different notes. For this reason, these are called major 'triads' ('tri' meaning 'three'). In a C chord these three notes are C, E and G. If we look at how these notes fit into the C major scale:

1	*2*	*3*	*4*	*5*	*6*	*7*	*8*
C	D	**E**	F	**G**	A	B	**C**

...we see that these notes are the first, the third and the fifth notes in the scale. And this is how we refer to the three notes in a major triad: the first, the third and the fifth. Sometimes the first is called the 'root', as it's the note that gives its name to the chord. Of, course the eighth note is also a C, but since this is simply the point at which the scale starts to repeat itself we don't call this the 'eighth'.

This applies to any basic major chord. For example, the three notes in an A chord are A, C# and E, and here is the A major scale:

1	*2*	*3*	*4*	*5*	*6*	*7*	*8*
A	B	**C#**	D	**E**	F#	G#	**A**

Don't worry about learning the notes in these scales or chords, I'm simply showing them so you can see how chords are constructed.

The three notes in a D chord are D, F# and A, and here is the D major scale:

1	*2*	*3*	*4*	*5*	*6*	*7*	*8*
D	E	**F#**	G	**A**	B	C#	**D**

On a piano keyboard it's possible to play triads with all of the notes in the order that they appear in a scale. For example, here is a C chord:

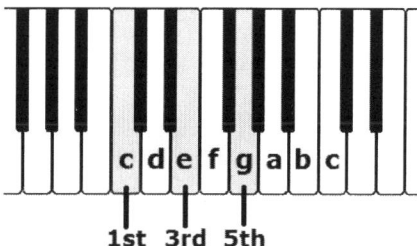

However, on string instruments like the ukulele, these notes often appear in a jumbled order. Have a look at these three uke chords:

- A Closer Look at Chords -

As there are four strings on the ukulele, notes in a chord are duplicated as well. Notice how in a C chord there are two firsts (a low C on the third string and a higher C on the first). In the A chord there are also two firsts (an A on the fourth string and an A with the same pitch on the first string). In the D chord there are two fifths (an A on the fourth string and an A with the same pitch on the first string).

Minor Chords
A minor chord is the same as a major chord, except that the third is flattened by one semitone. As one semitone equates to one fret, we just have to lower the third by one fret. This is straight forward with chords like Am and Dm (see below). Compare the fingering and notes within these chords with their major chord siblings above. With the A chord the C# has been flattened to a C, and with the D chord the F# has been flattened to an F.

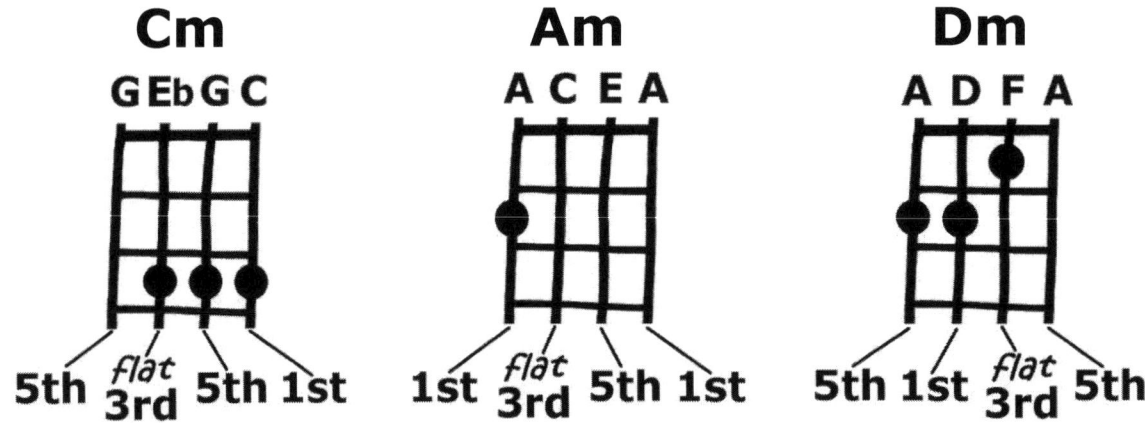

To turn the C into a Cm is a little more complicated. As the third in this major chord is made by an open second string, we cannot lower this note by one fret. Instead, we replace the first on the third string (the low C) with a flattened third (Eb), and replace the (non-flattened) third on the second string with a fifth (G) ...phew, that was complicated and perhaps a little confusing. A Cm is pretty easy to play though. You just make a bar across the first, second and third strings with your third finger.

- A Closer Look at Chords -

Seventh & 'major seventh' Chords
The sound and 'feel' of a basic major chord can be changed by adding extra notes. To turn a major chord into a seventh chord you might assume that we add the seventh note in the scale to the first, the third and the fifth that we already have. In fact, the 'seventh' note in these chords is actually a flattened seventh – that is, the note we add is one semitone (one fret) lower than the actual seventh note in the scale. For example, the seventh note in the C scale is B, therefore, to make a C7 chord we add a Bb. Here are the seventh forms of the C, A and D chords:

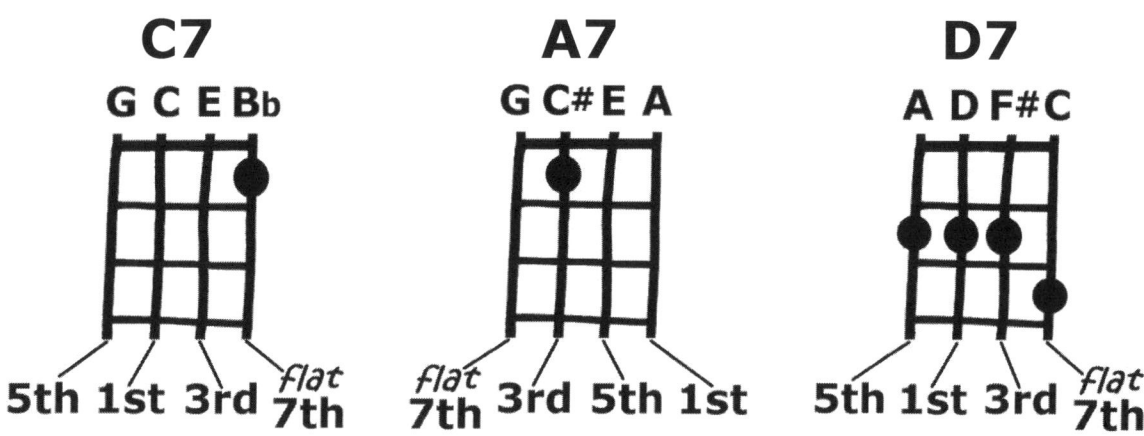

Compare these with the basic major chords, and you'll see that: with the C7, the flattened seventh has replaced the higher C; with the A7, the flattened seventh has replaced one of the two firsts; and with the D7, the flattened seventh has replaced one of the two fifths. Hence, in these chords there are no longer any duplicated notes.

If you add an actual seventh note to a major chord we create what is called a 'major seventh' chord (written as 'maj7'). Here are the major seventh forms of the C, A and D chords:

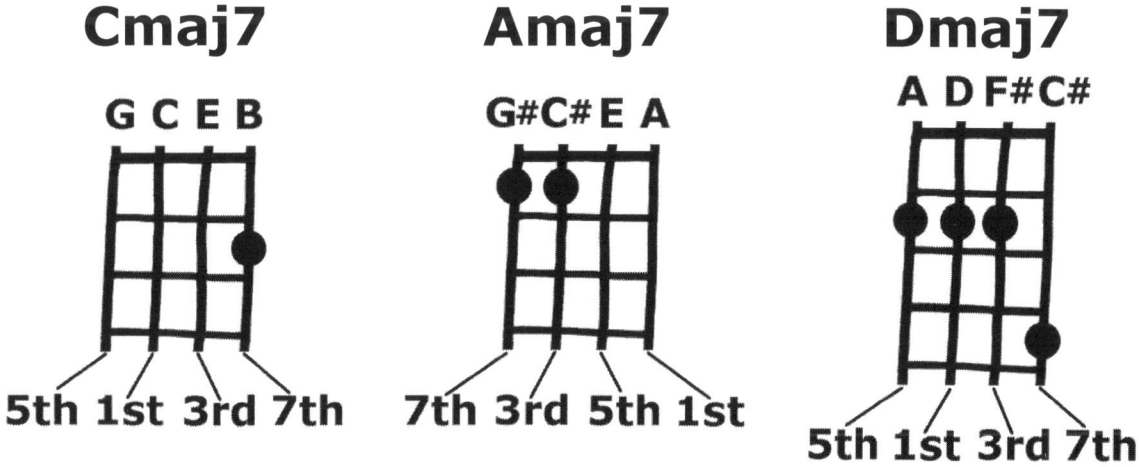

These look pretty similar to the seventh chords, except the seventh note in each instance is one fret higher. Major sevenths aren't used as often as seventh chords. I'd describe them as having a mellow, dreamy, jazzy feel to them. Play them and see for yourself. Indeed, all of the following chords tend to be thought of as 'jazz chords'.

A Closer Look at Chords

Sixth Chords

'Sixth chords' are constructed in just the same way as seventh and major seventh chords: the sixth note in the scale is added to the first, the third and the fifth note that make up the basic major chord. Here are the sixth versions of the C, A and D chords:

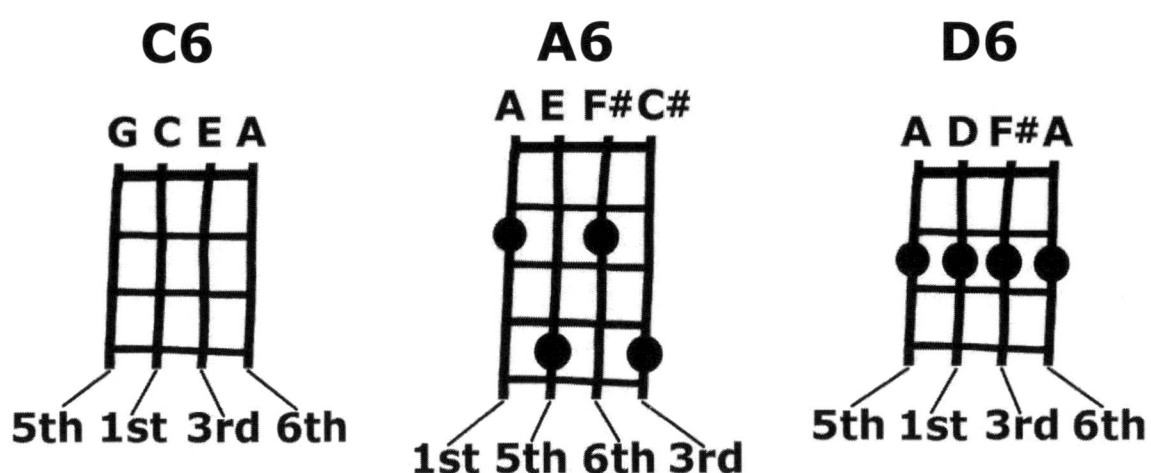

Once again, there are no duplicated notes in these chords.

You may think I've forgotten to add any dots to the C6 chord diagram, but that's actually how you play this chord ...with no fingers!

The A6 looks pretty tough to play, eh? To play this chord you make a bar across all of the strings on the second fret using your first finger, and make the notes on the fourth fret using your third finger on the third string and your fourth finger on the first string.

With the D6 you bar all of the strings with your first finger on the second fret. If we compare the D6 with the C6, we can see that all of the notes that make up the chord are in the same order. All of the notes in the D6 are simply one tone higher in pitch than those in the C6 ...it's pretty logical really, as D is one tone higher than C.

Like major seventh chords, sixth chords sound a little jazzy. In fact, they're often played as the very last chord in jazz, blues and rock 'n' roll songs. For example, when you come to the end of playing 'Hound Dog' (in the key of C), try strumming once on a C6 and letting the chord just ring. Sounds cool, eh?

- A Closer Look at Chords -

Minor Seventh Chords

As the name suggests, 'minor seventh' chords combine elements of both minor and seventh chords: the third is flattened by one semitone, and a flattened seventh note is added. Here are the minor seventh versions of the C, A and D chords:

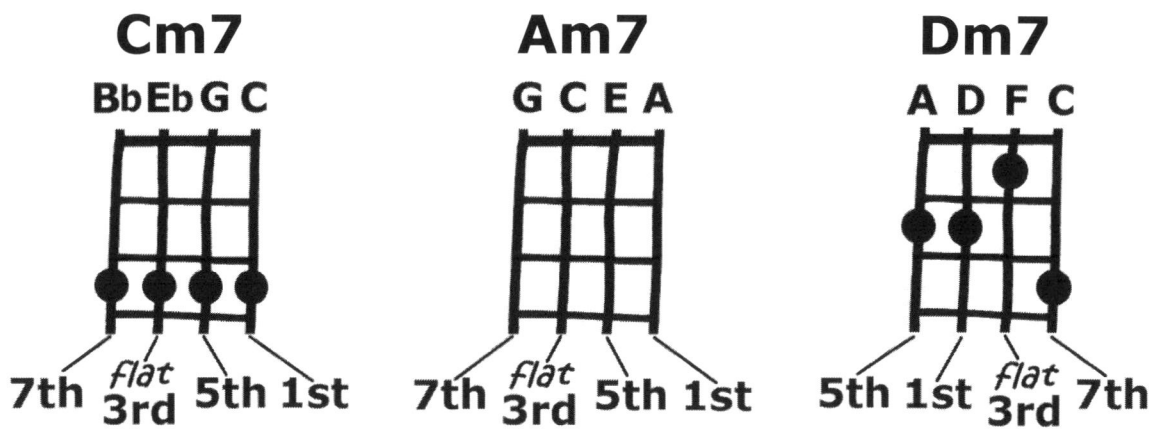

If you compare Am7 with C6, you'll notice something a little weird: these chords are exactly the same, except the notes making up the chord are labelled differently (and they're both played with no fingers!). This beggars the question: "If these two chords are fingered in exactly the same way, then how do we know what to call the chord when it appears in a song?" Well, without going into too much detail, what it's called will usually depend on the key of the song or where it appears in the song. In the end, it doesn't really matter which name you give it.

Notice how Cm7 has its component notes (the seventh, the flattened third, etc.) in the same order as with Am7 – all of the notes in Cm7 are simply one and a half tones higher in pitch than those in Am7. Again, this is quite logical, as a C is one and a half tones higher than an A.

If we compare Am7 with Am, we can see that a seventh has been added to the fourth string of the minor in just the same way as the seventh was added to the basic major chord. If we compare Cm7 with Cm, we can see that a seventh note has been added on the fourth string of the minor chord, replacing one of the two fifths. Similarly, if we compare Dm7 with Dm, we see that a seventh has been added to the first string of the minor chord in just the same way as the seventh was added to the basic major chord. Again, with Dm7 the seventh replaces one of two fifths.

Minor seventh chords combine the sad or tense feel of the minor with the additional, but different tension we get from the seventh. Again, these have a jazzy feel to them.

Ninth Chords

When there are only seven different notes in a major scale it may seem a little strange to have a chord called a 'ninth'. As we saw earlier, the eighth note in a scale is the same as the first, albeit an octave higher in pitch. Surely then, the ninth note is the same as the second, but an octave higher? Well, this is true. If you play a ninth chord on the piano, then the ninth is played eight notes above the first, and not just one note higher. This is why these chords are called 'ninths' and not 'seconds'.

This reasoning goes somewhat awry on the uke though. If you have a look at the chord diagrams below, you'll see that these ninth chords don't actually contain a first. This is because playing ninth chords doesn't just involve adding a ninth, it also involves adding a flattened seventh. Since there are only four strings on the uke, we cannot play these two added notes as well as the first, third and fifth. Hence, one of these notes from the basic major has to go. This is true of all ninth chords played on the uke. Compare each of these ninth chords with their basic major and seventh siblings to see where the ninths have been added.

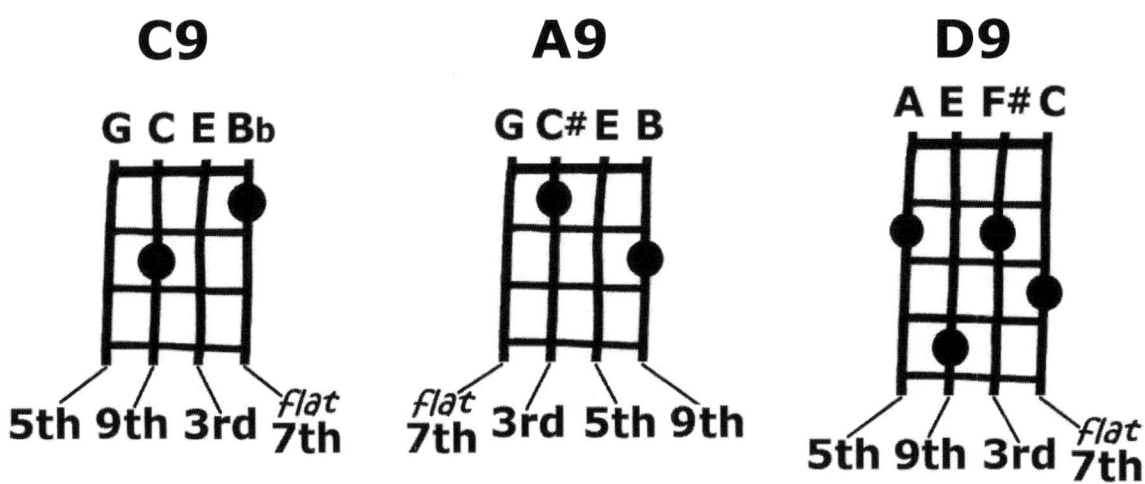

C9 is played with the first on the first string and the second finger on the third string. A9 is played with the first finger on the third string and the third finger on the first string. To play D9 you bar all of the strings on the second fret with your first finger, and play the C note on the first string with your second finger and the E note on the third string with your third finger.

Ninth chords are really useful if you want to play blues or jazz songs. For example, if you take a blues chord progression (such as the one shown below in the key of G) and play the 'four' (see 'Three Chord Tricks') as a ninth chord, you create a cool, bluesy/jazzy feel to the song you're playing. Note how the G chord (the 'one') is sometimes played as a seventh in this progression (this also adds to the bluesy/jazzy feel).

A Twelve-Bar Blues Chord Progression in the Key of G:

- A Closer Look at Chords -

Diminished and Augmented Chords
'Diminished' and 'augmented' chords are rather different to other types of chord: any note within the chord can be a first or root note ...I'll explain how this works:

Diminished Chords
Diminished chord shapes (sometimes identified by 'dim' and sometimes 'o') contain four different notes; hence, one chord shape can have four different names. A diminished chord comprises: a first, a flattened third, a flattened fifth (this is why it's called 'diminished'), and a sixth. Take a look at the Cdim, Adim and Ddim chords below.

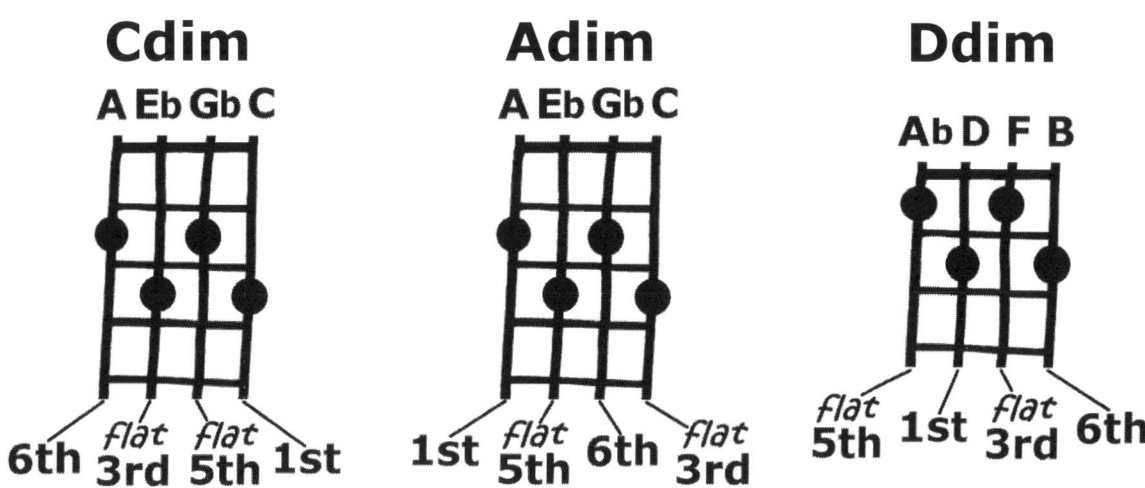

As can be seen, Cdim and Adim have exactly the same fingering. This chord shape contains a C and an A, and so, it can be either one of these chords. It also contains an Eb and a Gb, and so, it can be an Ebdim and a Gbdim too.

As the labels at the bottoms of the diagrams show, the 'roles' of the notes in the chord vary (i.e., whether they are considered a sixth, a flattened third or a flattened fifth) depending upon which note is taken to be the first (compare the Cdim with the Adim).

Notice how the Ddim (fingering shown on right) has the same shape as the Cdim and Adim, although it's played one fret lower on the fretboard. This chord could also be an Abdim, an Fdim or a Bdim.

So, with just two chord shapes we can play eight 'different' diminished chords. If this shape is moved one fret lower, so that it now looks like the chord on the right, we can play all twelve possible diminished chords. Of course, we run out of frets if we move the chord shape one fret lower, and so two of the notes (those on the second and fourth strings) are now played with open strings. This chord has been labelled as if it's C#dim, but it could also be considered a Gdim, an Edim or an A#dim.

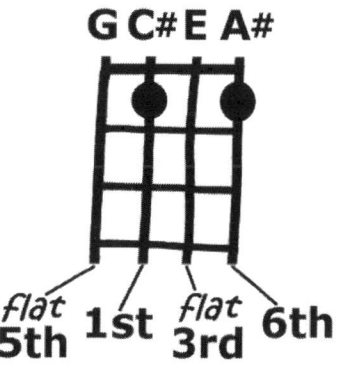

- 85 -

- A Closer Look at Chords -

The diagram below illustrates how it's possible for any of the four notes within the chord to be the first or root note.

All twelve possible notes are shown in ascending order of pitch running clockwise around the circle. The notes within a Cdim chord are indicated by the arrows. The first (C) appears at the top. Notice how each note is separated from its neighbours by three semitones and from the remaining note by six semitones. Whichever of the four notes in this chord we consider to be the first, this pattern will be exactly the same. In other words, the relative intervals (differences in pitch) between the notes in a diminished chord shape are exactly the same irrespective of which note is called the first/root.

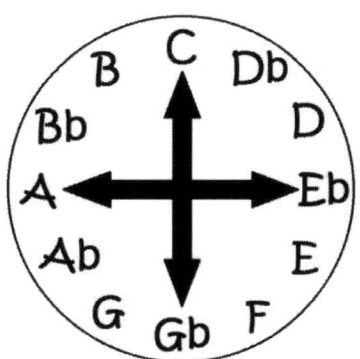

If you investigate diminished chords a little further, you'll see that proper diminished chords are actually 'triads' (i.e., three note chords), containing a first, a flattened third and a flattened fifth. "So why do the diminished chords we've been looking at have *four* different notes in them!" I hear you shout. Well, what ukulele and guitar players call 'diminished' chords are more accurately called 'diminished seventh' chords. If you take the seventh note in the scale, and flatten it twice (this is the seventh bit), then you get what might otherwise be called a sixth (as we've seen in the chord diagrams). As to why anyone would talk about a '*double* flattened seventh' and not a 'sixth' ...is beyond the scope of this guide.

Diminished chords have an ambiguous, bizarre sound. When you play them in isolation you might describe their sound as eerie, crazy or even annoying. They seem to leave the listener hanging ...needing resolution. Because of this, they're often used as transition or linking chords, or used to create a feeling of climax. For example, George Formby played a D#dim/Ebdim chord in the verses of his song 'When I'm Cleaning Windows'. Here's the first verse:

```
          C            C7
Now it's a job that just suits me
     F             D#dim
A window cleaner you would be
     C                C7 C6  C
If you can see what I can see
D#dim            C
When I'm cleanin' windows
```

Diminished chords are often used in jazz and classical music.

Augmented Chords

Augmented chords (sometimes identified by 'aug' and sometimes '+') contain three different notes (they're 'triads'); hence, as any note within the chord can be a first or root note, one chord shape can have three different names. An augmented chord comprises: a first, a third, and a sharpened fifth (this is why it's called an 'augmented' chord). However, as there are four strings on the ukulele, one of these notes is duplicated in the chord. Take a look at the Caug, Aaug and Daug chords below.

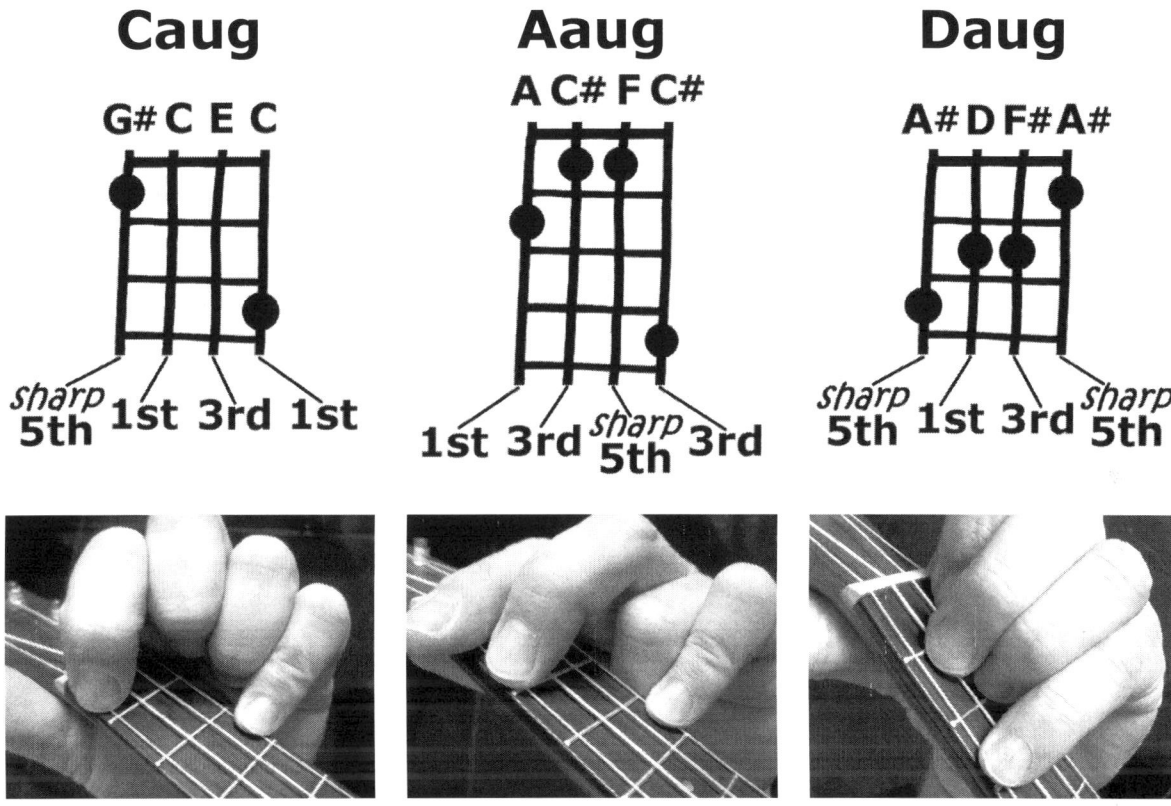

As can be seen, Caug has two firsts, Aaug has two thirds, and Daug has two sharpened fifths.

The Caug chord shape contains a G# and an E, and so, it can also be a G#aug and an Eaug. The A aug chord shape contains a C# and an F, and so, it can also be a C#aug and an Faug. The Daug chord shape contains an A# and an F#, and so, it can also be an A#aug and an F#aug.

As with diminished chords, the 'roles' of the notes in the chord vary (i.e., whether they are considered a third or a sharpened fifth) depending up which note is taken to be the first.

So, with just three chord shapes we can play nine 'different' augmented chords, and if the Daug shape is moved one fret higher (so that it's played on the second, third and fourth frets), we can play all twelve possible augmented chords.

- A Closer Look at Chords -

The diagram below illustrates how it's possible for any of the three different notes within the chord to be the first or root note.

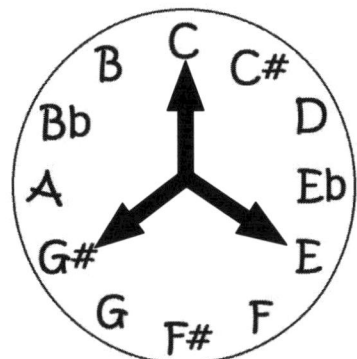

As before, all twelve possible notes are shown in ascending order of pitch running clockwise around the circle. The notes within a Caug chord are indicated by the arrows. The first (C) appears at the top. Notice how each note is separated from its neighbour by four semitones. Whichever of the three notes in this chord we consider to be the first, this pattern will be exactly the same. In other words, as with diminished chords, the relative intervals between the notes in a chord shape are exactly the same irrespective of which note is called the first/root.

Have a listen to Chuck Berry's recording of 'School Days' and you'll hear an augmented chord right at the beginning ...I think it sounds a like a bell ringing. Like diminished chords, augmented chords are often used as transition or linking chords. For example, you can hear an augmented chord in the chorus of The Beatles' 1963 song 'All My Loving'. Here it is in the key of C:

       Am   Eaug   C
All my loving I will send to you
       Am   Eaug   C
All my loving, darling I'll be true

Play these chords and you'll hear a lovely descending note effect on the fourth string. Augmented chords are often used in jazz and classical music.

"She loves uke, yeah, yeah, yeah!"

Why not join one of the many ukulele groups/clubs that are forming around the country? A comprehensive list of these can be found at www.gotaukulele.com. It's a great way to pick up playing tips, meet other ukulele players and even get to perform in public.

Above you can see eight members of AYUP! (All Yorkshire Ukulele Players) performing at Haworth in 2013.

18. Ukulele Chords

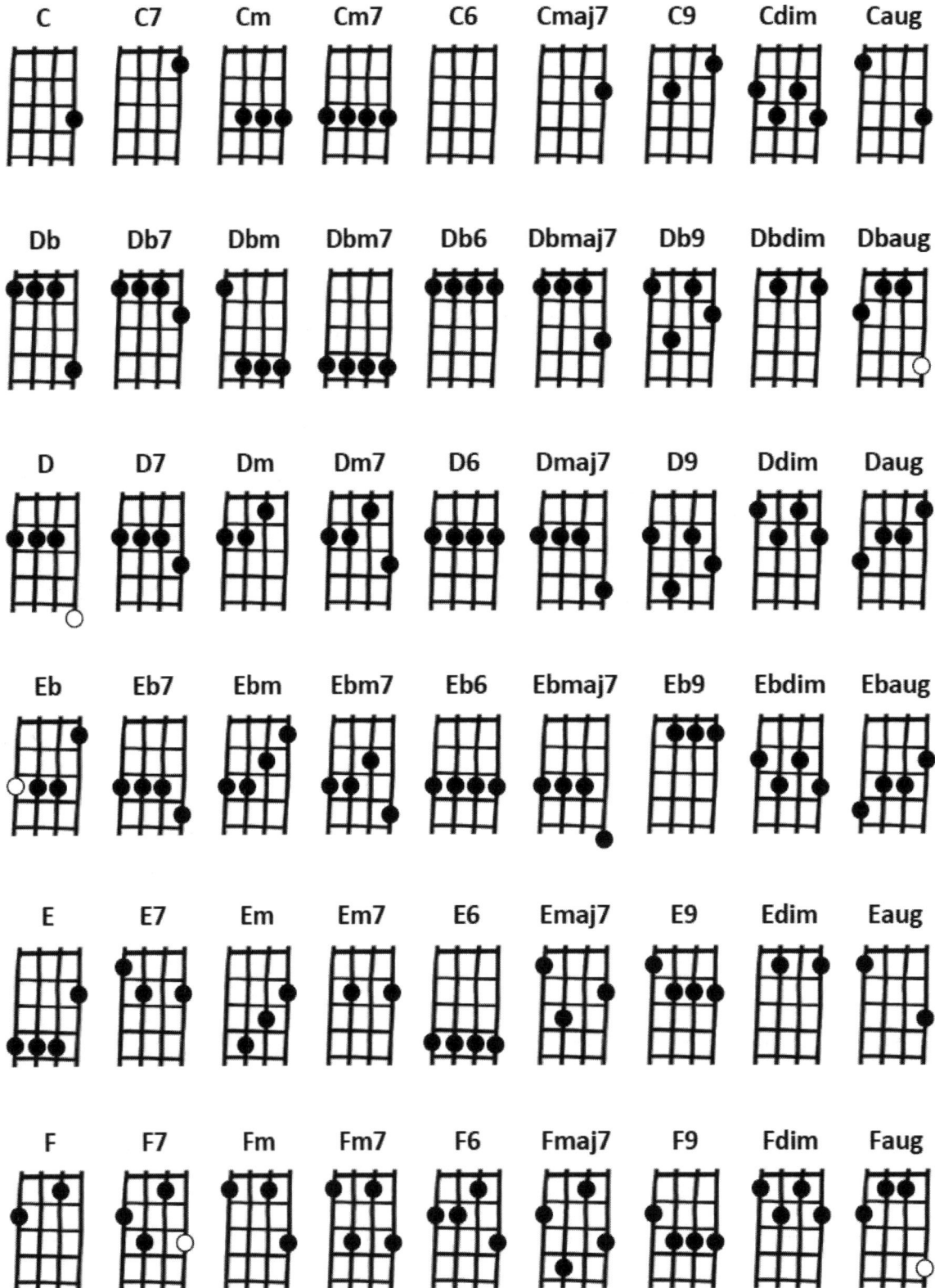

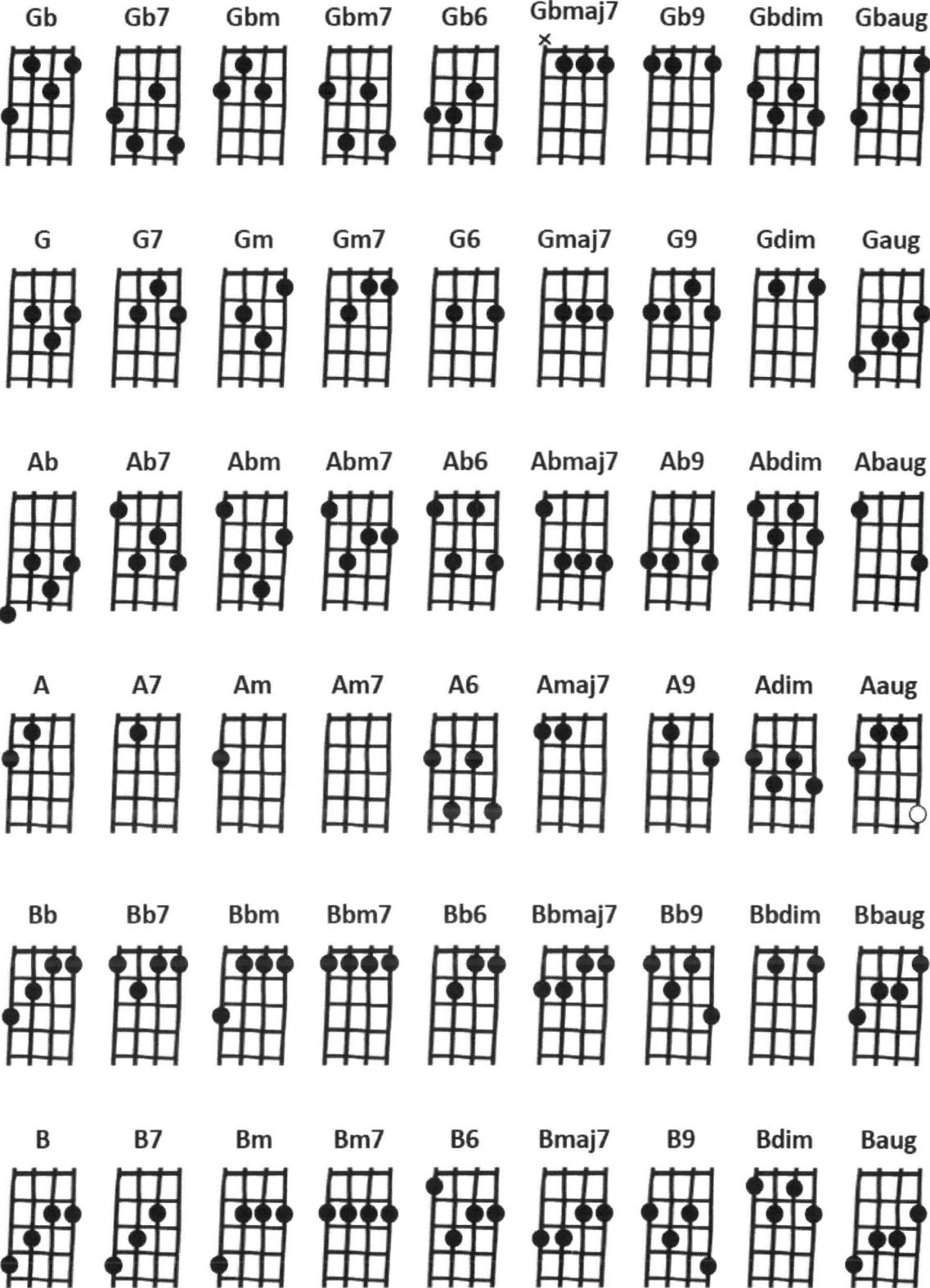